ENDORSEMENTS

"I'm fortunate to be surrounded by a staff who makes small groups for kids and teenagers a priority. That's why the principles discussed in *Creating a Lead Small Culture* resonate so deeply with our church. This is a timely work that provides a much needed blueprint for churches everywhere who believe kids and teenagers should be a priority in their ministry."

– MARK BATTERSON, NEW YORK TIMES BEST-SELLING AUTHOR AND LEAD PASTOR, NATIONAL COMMUNITY CHURCH

"After 14 years as a lead pastor, I'm convinced more than ever that a healthy church is built around making small groups a priority. If you don't connect kids and teenagers relationally with great leaders, you will sabotage the future and faith of a generation. That's why *Creating a Lead Small Culture* is such an important book for your team. It's a one-of-a kind manual to help every church create environments where kids can find a place to belong and someone who believes in the potential of their faith to change the world."

- PERRY NOBLE, SENIOR PASTOR, NEWSPRING CHURCH

"*Creating a Lead Small Culture* gives you more than just random ideas to help you do small groups better. It promotes proven strategies that actually work. If you are serious about discipleship and want to build a team of adults who invest weekly in teenagers, you need this book. So read it carefully, and get ready to rethink how you do student ministry. I learned a lot!"

- DOUG FIELDS, AUTHOR, SPEAKER, CO-FOUNDER DOWNLOADYOUTHMINISTRY.COM

"My wife Wendy and I have seen the benefits of small groups up close. Our daughter Jesse and our son Cole have been greatly influenced through small group leaders who share our values and yet speak to our kids from a different perspective. This has been a huge blessing to us as parents. As a pastor, I highly recommend *Creating a Lead Small Culture* to anyone who works with kids and teenagers. This is a smart, sustainable strategy with enormous generational impact."

- JEFF HENDERSON, LEAD PASTOR, GWINNETT CHURCH

"As a parent, leader, and researcher, my goal is that all kids will be surrounded by adults who lovingly help them be changed by Christ to change the world around them. This wise book gives your church the practical tools you need to make that goal a reality."

- KARA POWELL, PH.D., EXECUTIVE DIRECTOR OF THE FULLER YOUTH INSTITUTE (FYI)

"It's one thing to see the potential in small groups; it's another to create a church culture in which small groups thrive. *Creating a Lead Small Culture* is a must read for every senior leader and leadership team. In a masterful and engaging way, Reggie, Kristen and Elle explain the behaviors every team can incorporate into their culture to see kids, teens and families flourish through the ministry of the local church."

- CAREY NIEUWHOF, LEAD PASTOR, CONNEXUS COMMUNITY CHURCH

CREATING A LEAD SMALL CULTURE
Published by Orange
a division of The reThink Group, Inc.
5870 Charlotte Lane, Suite 300
Cumming, GA 30040 U.S.A.

The Orange logo is a registered trademark of The reThink Group, Inc.

All Scripture quotations, unless otherwise noted, are taken from The Holy Bible, New International Version®, NIV® Copyright © 1973, 1978, 1984, 2011 by Biblica, Inc.® Used by permission. All rights reserved worldwide. Other Orange products are available online and direct from the publisher. Visit www.OrangeBooks.com and www.ThinkOrange.com for more resources like these.

ISBN: 978-1-941259-08-5

©2014 Reggie Joiner, Kristen Ivy, and Elle Campbell

Authors: Reggie Joiner, Kristen Ivy, Elle Campbell
Editorial Team: Elizabeth Hansen, Mike Jeffries, Afton Manny, Tim Walker, Jennifer Wilder, Karen Wilson
Art Direction: Ryan Boon
Design: FiveStone

Printed in the United States of America
First Edition 2014

1 2 3 4 5 6 7 8 9 10

04/15/2014

CREATING A

LEAD SMALL
CULTURE

MAKE YOUR CHURCH A PLACE
WHERE KIDS BELONG

REGGIE JOINER

KRISTEN IVY   ELLE CAMPBELL

ABOUT THIS BOOK

For the past three years we have met with ministry leaders around the country to discuss one idea: how can age group ministries create a culture where small groups win? We met about it. We outlined it. We met about it some more. We taught it. We edited what we taught. We collected stories. We did a little more refining. Then, we wanted to put it into print. That doesn't mean we won't want to change it in a year or two, or maybe as soon as you email us with some new best practices. But for now, this is it. This is how we think you can create a lead small culture.

AUTHORS

When it came time to actually write *Lead Small Culture*, we were in a bit of a conundrum. With so many great leaders around the country weighing in on this idea how would we decide who put the words on paper? So, we drew straws. Okay, no. Since, we wanted a variety of experiences represented, we landed on three people who could bring three unique perspectives.

REGGIE JOINER @ReggieJoiner
Since someone on this writing team needed a little "experience," we thought maybe this was a good selection. Reggie has over 30 years of ministry experience leading teams who work with children and teenagers. As the family ministry director of North Point Ministries for 11 years, Reggie worked to build and refine a ministry that supported small groups for every age kid. Reggie is the founder and CEO of Orange, an organization whose purpose is to influence those who influence the next generation.

KRISTEN IVY @Kristen_Ivy
It's hard to talk about small groups without getting some input from a small group leader. (Have you ever noticed how some small group leaders have opinions about how small groups should work?) Kristen has 15 years of experience leading small groups of middle school and high school girls. Her opinions about creating a lead small culture come from years of reflecting on what ministry leaders can do to help the small group experience win. She has a Master's of Divinity and currently works as the executive director of messaging for Orange.

ELLE CAMPBELL @Ellllllllllle
We also needed a little expertise on YouTube sloth videos, which is why we selected Elle. That, and the fact that she has helped transition her middle school ministry at The Chapel at CrossPoint in Buffalo, New York, to one of the best lead small cultures we know. Elle has made recruiting, training and developing small group leaders her top priority. Her fresh ideas and energy keep us excited about everything that is still to come.

ARCHITECTS

These ministry leaders each have over 10 years of experience implementing a lead small culture. They have brainstormed, wrestled with, taught and evaluated the concepts in this book to make it what it is.

SUE MILLER @SueMiller01
PRESCHOOL/CHILDREN
Sue led preschool and children's environments (Promiseland) at Willow Creek Community Church for 17 years. After retiring from Willow, Sue joined the Orange staff in 2005. She continues to travel the world speaking and consulting with church leaders to help them reach the next generation. She is author of *Making Your Children's Ministry the Best Hour of Every Kids Week,* and co-author of *Parenting Is Wonder-full.* Sue loves to mentor leaders, inspire volunteers and consult with churches that strive to partner with parents.

CAREY NIEUWHOF @CNieuwhof
LEAD PASTOR
Carey is the lead pastor of Connexus Community Church, a growing multi-campus church near Toronto. Prior to starting Connexus in 2007, Carey served for 12 years in a mainline church, transitioning three declining congregations into one, rapidly growing congregation. He speaks to North American and global church leaders about change, leadership, and parenting. Author of *Leading Change Without Losing It,* and co-author of *Parenting Beyond Your Capacity,* Carey and his wife, Toni, live near Barrie, Ontario, and have two sons, Jordan and Sam.

KEVIN RAGSDALE
HIGH SCHOOL
Kevin Ragsdale serves on the leadership team and is the multi-campus high school director for North Point Ministries. As one of the first family ministry staff, Kevin developed the North Point student ministry philosophy to champion small groups. In addition to leading a staff that is responsible for over 2,000 high school students every week, Kevin also designs environments, oversees curriculum, roots for the Oklahoma Sooners, and plays hypercompetitive pickup basketball. Kevin is the co-author of *Make Believe: Five things great student pastors choose to believe.* Kevin and his wife Gina live in Cumming, Georgia, with their three children.

TERRY SCALZITTI @TScalzitti
LEAD PASTOR
Terry is the lead pastor of Ocean View Baptist Church in Myrtle Beach, South Carolina. In the few months since his arrival, the church has doubled in size. Known for his ability to connect with all types of audiences, Terry is passionate about reaching an unchurched culture. Previously, Terry was the associate pastor for adult and family ministries at First Baptist Fort Lauderdale where he and his team spent eight years transitioning to a lead small culture. He and his wife, Jennifer, have a son, Connor.

TOM SHEFCHUNAS @CoachShef
MIDDLE SCHOOL
Tom is the North Point Ministries multi-campus director of Transit (middle school). Tom's passion involves working with campus directors and their teams to recruit and develop the hundreds of small group leaders it takes to pull off Transit at five church campuses. Coauthor of *Lead Small*, Tom and his wife, Julie, live in Cumming, Georgia, with their three children, Mac, Joey and Cooper.

CONTRIBUTORS

These ministry leaders are currently working in churches to create a lead small culture. They live out the beliefs and behaviors of this book every week. As you read, you will see examples from their real world practical experience. Use these bios to see which leaders are in a context similar to yours.

CASS BRANNAN @CassBrannan
PRESCHOOL
Cass is a groups director in Waumba Land at Buckhead Church, in Atlanta, Georgia. Cass graduated from Georgia Southern University and Southeastern Seminary. He's passionate about helping churches influence preschoolers and their families. Cass loves to do anything outside including but not limited to walking, running, playing ultimate Frisbee, biking, or whatever he can do with his four amazing boys and wife, Mary Beth.

ABBEY CARR @OrangeAbbey
ELEMENTARY
Abbey has been involved in children's ministry for over 12 years, both as a ministry director and a volunteer. She currently works for Orange, developing relationships with church leaders and helping them win in their elementary environments. Abbey has served as an SGL for 4th and 5th grade girls, and looks forward to leading a new group of Kindergarteners this fall with her daughter, Lillian.

KENNY CONLEY @KennyConley
ALL AGES/MULTISITE
Kenny has been in children's ministry for 15 years, and is currently serving as the NextGen pastor at Gateway Church in Austin, Texas. His passion to see the next generation come to know and follow Christ propels him to constantly rethink how the church approaches ministry to kids and their families. Three places Kenny wants to visit before he dies include Antarctica, the summit of Kilimanjaro, and Advanced Base Camp of Mount Everest.

DEXTER CULBREATH @Dextext
ELEMENTARY
Dexter is the "VicKids" elementary director at Victory World Church in Norcross, Georgia. He's had the privilege of working with children, teens, and families for many years and has an outrageous passion for relationships. He might also have an outrageous passion for giving everyone he meets a nickname.

ADAM DUCKWORTH @Adam_Duckworth
ELEMENTARY
Adam currently serves as the family pastor at First Baptist Fort Lauderdale. At First Baptist, he played a critical role in their transition from a Sunday school model to a lead small culture. Adam also has over 1,100 Disney Vinylmations and sees no end in sight.

AMY FENTON @AmyMFenton
ELEMENTARY
For 18 years, Amy served as a children's pastor at The People's Church in Franklin, Tennessee and then The Church at Brook Hills in Birmingham, Alabama, leading a team of over 300 volunteers. Currently, Amy travels the country coaching church leaders and volunteers. Amy could eat peanut butter chocolate ice cream from Baskin Robbins daily.

MATT IVY @TheMattIvy
HIGH SCHOOL
Matt has lead middle school and high school small groups for the past 10 years. As an XP3 Orange Specialist, Matt spends most days talking to student leaders about their ministry strategy and curriculum. If you grab him a quad, tall Americano with two raw sugars, you'll probably be best friends.

DR. DARREN KIZER @DarrenKizer
ALL AGES/MULTISITE
Darren was executive pastor of family ministries at Parker Hill Community Church for 11 years. At Parker Hill, he lead staff and volunteer teams for three campuses. Darren also invests in NextGen leaders through consultation, education, and writing. He and his wife Becky live in Scranton, Pennsylvania— where the TV show *The Office* was set.

BROOKLYN LINDSEY @BrooklynLindsey
MIDDLE SCHOOL
Brooklyn began working with teenagers in 1997 as a volunteer and
became a full-time youth pastor in 2001. She currently works with middle
schoolers at Highland Park Church of the Nazarene in Lakeland, Florida.
Without her two little girls, Kirra and Mya, she probably wouldn't have
much of an Instagram account.

GINA MCCLAIN @Gina_McClain
ELEMENTARY/MULTISITE
Gina started on staff at LifeChurch.tv in 1999 where she remained for over
a decade. Currently, Gina is the children's pastor at Faith Promise Church
in Knoxville, Tennessee. Having led in two large multi-site churches in the
past 14 years, Gina is even more convinced that relationships are not only
vital, but the only sustainable way to reach kids.

BOBBI MILLER @BobbiMiller17
ELEMENTARY
Bobbi began full-time ministry at Willow Creek Community Church 23
years ago. After her time at Willow, Bobbi joined the world of kid's
ministry in a small church setting in Michigan, and is now on staff at Bent
Tree Bible Fellowship. Bobbi's husband, Paul, is also on staff at Bent Tree,
and the two of them get to practice leading small every day at home with
their small group of five kids.

LATASHA MORRISON @LatashaMorrison
ELEMENTARY
Latasha is currently the children's director at First Evangelical Free Church
of Austin, Texas. Previously, she was the NextGen director for a church in
Atlanta, Georgia, overseeing everything from the cradle to the career in a
6,000-member church. Currently, Latasha lives in Austin, Texas, where she
recently completed her Master's in Business from Liberty University.

KATHIE PHILLIPS @KidMinspiration
ELEMENTARY
Kathie has served in children's ministry since age 13 and has spent six of
the last eight years overseeing ministry in both small and larger church
environments. She currently serves as director of children's ministry at
Central Presbyterian Church in Baltimore, Maryland. In her spare time,
she enjoys traveling, reading, and watching episodes of her favorite TV
show—the original *Beverly Hills, 90210*.

NINA SCHMIDGALL @NinaSchmidgall
ALL AGES/MULTISITE
Nina serves as director of family ministry at National Community Church in Washington, DC. While working in the nation's capital as a legislative director in the House of Representatives, writing and directing education and family policy, Nina realized her passion for strengthening the family and the home. She has overseen the family ministry department at NCC since 2001. In that time, NCC has grown their children's programs to seven locations.

JEFF WALLACE @IAmJeffWallace
HIGH SCHOOL
Jeff is an urban ministry innovator, author, and leader. He serves as pastor of youth development at Peace Baptist Church in Decatur, Georgia, where he oversees all of the children, teen, and young adult ministries. Jeff enjoys doing life with his wife Quovadis and three boys, Jeffrey, Christopher, and Cameron.

JEREMY ZACH @JeremyZach
MIDDLE SCHOOL/HIGH SCHOOL
Jeremy started student ministry in 2002 at Bethany Church in Los Angles, a church of about 500. In 2010, he joined the XP3 Students team as an Orange Specialist, and is currently a middle school small group leader at Browns Bridge Community church. He loves cats.

JENNY ZIMMER @JenZim15
PRESCHOOL
Jenny is the family life director, and the director of FX and preschool environments at Discovery Church in Simi Valley, California. She's been doing ministry for over 10 years. Jenny has what she considers four children, although not everyone may see it that way; she has two daughters and two Cocker Spaniels who are her babies.

A NOTE ABOUT AFTON @aftonsaid
Afton Manny is the glue that holds Lead Small together. When there is a meeting, she is there. When ideas have to be captured in notes, she is there. When we had the idea to make an app to help small group leaders win . . . well, Afton's life got very busy. We would like to thank Afton for— in her own words—having ears that "perk up like a dog when someone says, 'Lead Small.'" Afton: You not only make this happen. You keep it fun. (Disclaimer: This Twitter account will not help you lead small. But it might make you laugh.)

TABLE
OF
CONTENTS

CULTURE:

the beliefs and behaviors
that define a social group

These pages explore the beliefs, behaviors, and habits that drive leaders who make small groups a priority.

These leaders share a common conviction that kids and teenagers need other adults besides their parents.

They need other adults . . .
who believe in God.
who believe in them.
and who give them a place to belong.

That's why we wrote this book.

We are not claiming
it answers every question
or solves every problem.

But it will give you more ideas on how to effectively
create a culture where kids can connect relationally.

If you want to influence what kids believe about
God, themselves, and the rest of the world,
then give them somewhere to belong.

That's why we also hope you will
join this conversation and champion the belief that relationships
with kids and teenagers should be a priority in our churches.

GIVE THEM SOMEWHERE

I love nouns. It's probably because nouns were the easiest things for me to identify when I (Reggie) had to diagram sentences for Miss McGuffey's class in high school. Nouns are simple. They are just a person, place, or thing. They're not nearly as confusing as adverbs, participles, or dangling modifiers. (Make sure you don't use that last term in front of middle schoolers.) I'm glad that nouns are clear, tangible, and concrete.

What does that have to do with creating a place for kids to belong? A lot. We think kids and teenagers need two important nouns in their life. They need *someone* and they need *somewhere*.

Before anyone can wrestle with abstract concepts like faith, hope, and the meaning of life, they simply need to know who loves them and where they belong. In my early days, I tried to hand students a list of action verbs before I handed them a few solid nouns. I think I forgot that in the English language, nouns usually come before verbs. Since then I have learned that before you can expect kids to believe, you usually need to give them someone who believes in them. Before you ask teenagers to "go tell the world," you need to give them a safe place where they know they belong.

KIDS NEED **TWO** IMPORTANT **NOUNS** SO THEY CAN ANCHOR THEIR LIVES TO SOMETHING SOLID.

....

They need a
PERSON

They need a
PLACE

....

Research suggests the earlier they identify the "who"s and "where"s of their life, the more solid their faith will be. That's where you come in as a ministry leader. You can't force or determine the faith or future of anyone, really. The only thing you can actually do is recruit leaders and establish places so kids can know they belong somewhere.

Never underestimate the power the right place has to affect relationships. Think of some of the best friendships you have observed. There was probably a significant gathering place that became the iconic symbol of the relationship.

Seinfield had a diner.
Friends had a coffee house.
Cheers had a bar.

Okay. Those may not be the best examples of relationships. But they all speak to the power of having a place "where everybody knows your name." If you want to get serious about influencing the hearts of this generation, you have to think about creating an actual, visible, consistent place where they know they belong.

When it comes to designing environments, no organization has more opportunity than the church. Unfortunately, some of us have insisted for a long time the Church is not a place, but rather it's people. Maybe we have forgotten that people still need a place and realistically, the Church is both.

For nearly two thousand years the Church has met in homes, catacombs, restaurants, buildings, cathedrals, tents, theatres, town halls, coffeehouses, storefronts, schools, and hotels. What do all these have in common besides the fact that they are all nouns? They were actual physical places where groups of people could meet. Regardless of your denomination or worship style, the local church has always been a place where people could sit down and engage in a learning and worship experience.

The point is you need a place.

Regardless of how you define the church, you can't ignore that one of its primary functions is to make it easier for people to assemble. The church has always involved a location. Ideally, the church may be made up of people, but practically the church has to assume a responsibility to establish a place where multiple people can actually meet.

Think about it this way:
The church can't force people to follow Jesus.
The church can't demand that people embrace the gospel.
The church can't dictate that everyone connects relationally.

But the church *can* create a safe and relevant place for people to engage, learn, and connect. Just remember that every church, regardless of its size or budget, can create an environment that makes it easier for kids and teenagers to experience authentic relationships.

One of the most important things your staff should do as a team is prioritize which place is most important in your church. Some churches have so many programs or environments it's easy to have competing systems that confuse people and dilute their potential to influence a kid's faith. That's why we think every church should ask this critical question, Where do you want someone to be?

If we amplified this question, we could say it in a number of ways.

Where do you want kids to ultimately be so you can influence their faith and character?

What is the most optimal environment in your church where kids have the best potential to grow in their relationship with Jesus Christ?

If every week, kids or teenagers can only show up one time, experience one environment, participate in one activity, where would you tell them to go?

Every church needs to ask and answer questions like these if they hope to lead kids to a more authentic faith. Since you have limited resources, volunteers, and time, it's simply important to prioritize which environment in your church is most important. It's difficult to lead kids somewhere if you don't know where you are leading them. So, what is your answer to the question, "Where do you want kids to be?"
Is it Sunday school?
Is it children's church?
Or is it Activate Live? (The weekly program for your teenagers—not the yogurt).

You need to decide. Until you do, you can't really be strategic in how you organize your ministry. We think the best answer to the question is to ask another question.

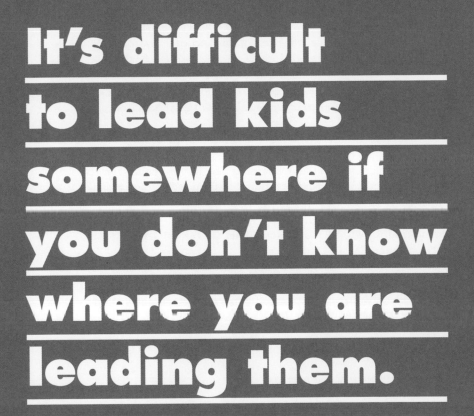

It's difficult to lead kids somewhere if you don't know where you are leading them.

Which environment connects a small group of kids with a consistent leader?

(If we were in a restaurant eating lunch, this is when we would draw a dot and a circle to represent a small group and a leader.)

Generally speaking, we use these terms to clarify two big ideas:

Small group: *a consistent gathering of a few for the purpose of growing in their relationship with God and each other.*

Small group leader (SGL): *someone who chooses to invest in the lives of a few to encourage authentic faith.*

So, if you ask us the question, "Where do you want kids or teenagers to be?" Our answer will be, "In a small group." You can pick a different answer, but just remember: everything else in your culture will be affected by how you respond to this question. When you create a lead small culture, you establish a priority with everyone in your ministry that everything you do should somehow point to small groups. Therefore, small groups become the primary focus of your ministry strategy.

When a lead small culture is established, it tends to simplify how you evaluate success and how you communicate what is important. There are two basic indicators that prove you have actually made small groups a focus in your church.

1. SMALL GROUPS BECOME AN ANSWER TO EVERYTHING.

- How do we disciple kids and teenagers?
- How do we nurture an ongoing relationship with parents?
- How do we plug students into service opportunities?
- How do we evaluate what is working in our ministry?
- How do we give someone a sense of belonging?
- How do we monitor what is happening in kids' weekly lives? GPS tracking devices maybe or . . .

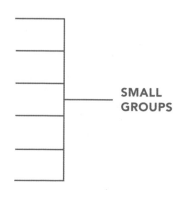

SMALL GROUPS

2. SMALL GROUP BECOMES THE ANSWER EVERYWHERE.

You'll know that you've made small groups the focus when every age group pastor or ministry leader also has the same answer. Remember that too many different answers usually indicates nobody knows the answer. That's why a lead small culture tends to put everyone on the same page and creates synergy with the team. Not only should all roads lead to small groups, but all voices should as well. Alignment on a team will make a critical difference in your church. When everyone on your staff is saying the same thing, it will move everyone in your church in the same direction.

....

IF SMALL GROUPS BECOME THE PRIMARY PLACE YOU WANT KIDS AND TEENAGERS TO BE, THEN THAT WILL ULTIMATELY CHANGE HOW YOU POSITION A LOT OF WHAT YOU DO.

....

It will change how you do PROGRAMMING.

You will start evaluating your programs on the basis of whether they complement or compete with groups.

You will tweak programs so they can move people to a small group more effectively, and you will learn to stop doing things that don't really lead anywhere.

You will shift from creating special events or camps for just kids or teenagers individually to an emphasis on events for small groups to attend together.

It will change how you work as a TEAM.

You will reorganize your staff to make sure someone is focused on making small groups win.

You will hire or recruit organizational leaders who think more strategically about how to arrange groups and track progress.

You will see the advantage of having consistent meetings for various age group directors or pastors to improve the overall small group structure.

It will change how you recruit VOLUNTEERS.

You will make sure the average volunteer understands specifically how their role helps small groups win.

You will elevate those who volunteer to lead small groups as the most critical in your organization.

You will mobilize teenagers to partner with adults to lead small groups of preschoolers and kids.

It will change how you create ENVIRONMENTS.
You will leverage every platform to promote and explain how to connect in small groups.
You will draw a clearer distinction between teaching a class and discipling kids.
You will evaluate presentations and curriculum on the basis of how they affect the activity and connection within the small group.

It will change how you partner with FAMILIES.
You will position your small group leaders to have relational influence with parents.
You will invite parents into a strategic partnership with small groups so they know they have an advocate for their family.
You will think about ways to resource both leaders and parents to synchronize them in a comprehensive strategy for kids and teenagers.

When you create a lead small culture, you tend to move things around in your organization so everything points to small groups. It's interesting how simply re-arranging the furniture in a room can enhance or inhibit how people relate and connect. But that's one of your principal jobs as a next generation leader. So hopefully, these next chapters will help you sharpen your skills—

- To architect and design better environments.
- To create places where kids have a better chance to connect relationally.
- To re-arrange the furniture so every kid and teenager has a seat at the table.

Every kid needs a PERSON and they need a PLACE.

Just remember: as a leader, you are responsible to give kids the nouns they need to grow personally. You may be the best chance they will ever have to find somewhere to belong.

Give them somewhere to belong.

GIVE THEM SOMEONE

Do kids really need to belong before they can believe? Is it necessary to re-arrange your ministry to make sure teenagers have a place where they are known and people who know them? We think so. We actually think a small group is one of the best ways to introduce this generation to the concept of a God who loves them unconditionally. Think about it.

You can't see God.

I have never seen God, and neither have you.

Okay. Maybe you think you have. But I'm going to bet it wasn't actually God. More than likely you were staring too long at a cloud formation, or you drank too much Nyquil. The point is there are no tangible, verifiable images you can hold up and say, "This is God."

It's too bad social media didn't exist thousands of years ago. It would have settled a lot of issues for skeptics.

Imagine if . . .
Moses sent a pic of God writing the Ten Commandments.
Peter uploaded images of Jesus walking on the water.
John posted video of Jesus ascending into heaven on YouTube.

(If social media had been around, it could have settled that whole dinosaur debate, too.)

Your job as a pastor or Christian leader would be a lot easier if those moments had been captured with some actual digital images.

Instead, you probably spend a lot of time trying to convince kids or teenagers to pursue a God they have never seen. It's tricky. God doesn't have a Twitter account or a Facebook page. So, how do you invite people to follow someone they can't touch, or see, or hear? And how do you move them toward an authentic and personal faith in a God who may seem distant, vague, and unpredictable?

How do you move them toward an authentic and personal faith in a God who may seem distant, vague, and unpredictable?

We have watched hundreds of churches debate which strategy is best for children and teenagers. We have listened to confident leaders promote their interpretation of biblical truth and advocate their version of church as the solution for the dying faith of a generation. And while ministry leaders may not agree on every detail, we are connected by a common mission to help kids and adults grow in their relationship with Jesus Christ.

So, back to the question.
How do you build authentic faith in kids and teenagers?
We think we have finally discovered the answer.
And it's really simple.

Just kidding.

The truth is, it will never be simple. That's the nature of faith and pursuing a relationship with a mysterious and majestic Creator. We aren't writing this book because we think we have the answer, but because we have made a number of key observations through the years about kids and faith. Here are a few:

- You don't shape a kid's faith by teaching them doctrine. (Whatever you talk them into, someone else can talk them out of.)

- You don't shape a kid's faith by persuading them to have better standards. (They may ultimately *give* up if they feel like they can't *measure* up.)

- You don't shape a kid's faith by getting them to attend your events. (At some point, they will compare the quality of your production to what culture produces, and you will probably lose.)

....

BUT YOU CAN SHAPE A KID'S FAITH BY CONNECTING THEM TO CARING ADULTS WHO WILL BE PRESENT IN THEIR LIFE.

Are we saying theology, lifestyle, and church attendance don't matter? Not at all. But we are suggesting any of those things, without caring and consistent relationships, will have a limited impact. You don't have to look very far to find sobering stats about the number of teenagers and college students who have walked away from church.

Our experience suggests that most kids who grow up and leave church did not run away from caring relationships. They ran away from
prejudice
judgment
irrelevance
and religion.

For the past twenty years, I (Reggie) have been able to hang out with a distinctive group of college students during the summer. They are the interns who show up to help at summer camps and they represent a group of college-age individuals who didn't walk away from faith. Instead, they decided to use their summer breaks to invest in the faith of teenagers.

I'm always curious about their stories and what helped shape their faith to this point. At the beginning of the summer, I traditionally take them through an exercise. I ask them to pinpoint a few things in their past that contributed to their spiritual growth. Then, we write those things down on index cards, put them on a creative board, and look for similar patterns in their stories. For nearly two decades the results have been the same. Every defining moment in their stories always comes back to one or more of these five issues.

> *Life-changing truths* – change how they see themselves or God
> *Spiritual disciplines* – help them connect personally to God
> *Ministry opportunities* – increase their sense of mission
> *Pivotal circumstances or events* – compel them to rethink their priorities
> *Significant relationships* – help them navigate their spiritual journey

One of the most enlightening moments of these sessions with our camp interns is always the point when we scan the board for the names of people who have impacted their lives. **In everyone's story of faith, there are people who have shown up and become catalysts for their spiritual growth.** Think about it. If you are reading this right now, chances are you believe what you believe and you do what you do because of the way someone influenced your faith. More than likely, it wasn't just one person, but several. You could probably write down a short list of people who have been strategic influences in your life.

Just like the people in ancient times developed their view of God as . . .
the God of Abraham
the God of Isaac
or the God of Moses,

You have developed a sense of who God is because you have met . . .
the God of Susan
the God of Carlos
or the God of Jeff.

God uses people. That's the point. He always has. Sometimes we forget the God of the Bible is the God of the *people* of the Bible. God has always used people to demonstrate His story of redemption.

The essence of our faith is linked to the idea that God actually became human. He became one of us. So we could . . .
touch Him.
hear Him.
see Him.

God simply decided the most effective way
to redeem us was to become one of us.

The narrative of the Bible is anchored to the fact that God became a man so He could prove how much He loves us. And that Jesus literally became human. What happened on the cross and at the resurrection is so significant that sometimes we fail to recognize what God did just by showing up as a person.

He became us.
Not a book.
Not a really cuddly looking animal.
Not a supernatural being from Ezekiel's vision.
But a real, live, breathing human being.

So, what's the point of all of this? As believers, it's possible to get so caught up in our sermons, ordinances, doctrines, spiritual disciplines, and church programs that we forget the character of God was revealed to an ancient culture through an actual person. Turn that one over in your head when you can't fall asleep at night. Evidently, God saw the need to show who He is to people who couldn't see Him by sending someone they could see.

God saw the need to show who He is to people who couldn't see Him by sending someone they could see.

The incarnation is one of the most complicated, paradoxical truths of our Christian faith. Jesus was as much man as if He were not God at all, and as much God as if He were not man at all. He was God and man at the same time. He stepped onto the planet so we could see God. This is what makes our faith different from most other religions. We follow a man who believed He was God. He actually said things like, "Anyone who has seen me has seen the Father." Of course, that statement raised a few eyebrows with the religious leaders. They charged Him with blasphemy, convicted Him of a capital crime, and executed Him. The only problem: He was God, so He didn't stay dead.

Of course, because He was God, He accurately predicted He would be killed and then come back to life. For some reason, everyone was surprised when He actually did—but don't judge them too quickly. Sometimes it's just easier to understand things when we're looking backward. It kind of makes sense that what Jesus said before He died became a little clearer to the disciples after He came back to life.

When you read what Jesus says and you believe He actually came back to life, it gives His words a little extra punch. So, if you think something He said seems a little unreasonable or impossible, just remember—He was dead and now He's alive!

With that in mind, here's one of His statements that seems a little outlandish:

"Very truly I tell you, whoever believes in Me will do the works I have been doing, and they will do even *greater* things than these, because I am going to the Father. . . . And I will ask the Father, and He will give you another advocate to help you and be with you forever—the Spirit of truth." **John 14:12, 16-17a, NIV**

Sounds a little crazy, doesn't it? When He left, Jesus promised to send His Spirit to be here with us. Maybe that explains why He prayed such an unusual prayer,

"Father, just as you are in Me and I am in You. May they (those who are followers of Jesus) also be in us *so that the world may believe* that You have sent Me. . . . *Then the world will know that you sent Me and have loved them even as You have loved Me,"* **John 17: 21b, 23b, NIV**

Did you get it? Jesus, the God Man, the Man God, who died and rose again, predicted that one day the world will know He loves them, even though they *can't see* Him, because they *can see* the people who are following Him.

....

Please don't miss this.

PEOPLE CAN'T SEE GOD.
PEOPLE CAN'T SEE JESUS.
PEOPLE CAN'T SEE THE HOLY SPIRIT.

BUT PEOPLE CAN SEE PEOPLE WHO FOLLOW GOD.
PEOPLE CAN SEE THE CHURCH.

....

That's why what you do, as a pastor or leader, is so important. The church has been part of God's strategy for a long time.

The best chance someone may have to personally see God is to get a close-up look at the people who follow God.

That's why your mission is simple, but complicated. You're supposed to do what Jesus did. Show up in the lives of others so they can see God. Engage with broken people so they can believe in the Jesus who bled for them. That's why the work of your church is so critical. You are called to do more than simply make a presentation of the gospel. You are called to engage in the messiness of humanity *because* of the gospel. You are compelled by the Spirit of Christ in you to convince your world that *God* loves them by the way *you* love them. The fact is, the Church is one of the most divinely strategic organizations that exists. But when or if a church fails to make relationships a priority, it risks becoming irrelevant.

So, let's settle it. God wired your faith to be shaped and influenced by someone else's faith. And God designed you to love people in such a way they can see Him working in you.

Regardless of the style or size of your church, your greatest asset to building faith in the next generation is not your Bible study, worship band, facilities, or budget. The most valuable resources you have to help people see God are the people in your church who know God.

The most valuable resources you have to help people see God are the people in your church who know God.

And if you hope to help a generation of kids and teenagers know God, then you have to be strategic about how you connect them to small group leaders who believe in God and who believe in them. We'll talk more about the role of your small group leaders later, but for now, let's just agree that every kid needs someone who believes in God and who believes in them.

When *Fortune* magazine released "The World's 50 Greatest Leaders" in 2014, Geoffrey Canada was number twelve on the list. Canada has been someone we have respected for years because of his work with children and teenagers. A few years ago, we had the privilege of meeting with him. Canada is an education reformer who grew up in the South Bronx, went to Harvard graduate school, and came back to Harlem as the president and CEO of the Harlem Children's Zone. He has dedicated his life to giving disadvantaged kids a better chance by helping them graduate high school and get into college. In a conversation with Geoffrey, he made an interesting observation about the kids in Harlem. He said the reason so many of these kids don't believe in God is because they've never seen adults who are God-like. What he was saying was simple—in order to believe in a good and creative God who loves them in spite of their mistakes and their mess, kids and teenagers need adults who will do the same.

We know recruiting SGLs to invest weekly in the lives of kids is not the only thing you have to do as leader, but we do believe it is the most important thing you do. We hope you are reading this book because you believe that, too. If you don't, we hope you will by the time you finish.

Our premise is simple.
Leaders who connect with kids in a SMALL group over time have the potential to make a BIG impact on their faith.

That's why we challenge leaders to **lead small.**
When you **lead small,** you simply make a choice to invest strategically in the lives of a few over time so you can help them build authentic faith. When you lead small, you realize that what you do for a few will always have more potential than what you do for many.

So if you want kids to know God, maybe one of the most important things you can do is to give them someone who will talk with them, hang out with them, and do life with them.

The best way to help kids know God is to connect them with someone who knows God.

ACT LIKE YOU BELIEVE IT

How you behave has a direct effect on what you believe.
And what you believe has a definite impact on how you behave.

Sometimes it's hard to know which one is driving the patterns you see in your organization. But they both have profound influence in your culture.

I (Reggie) remember listening to a lead pastor of a church explain how he had built his church. At one point in the message he actually stated, "We don't do small groups at our church. We tried them, and they just didn't work." The speaker who followed him was a friend of mine, and I smiled when he responded by saying, "He's right, I have been to his church and groups don't work at *his* church." He knew what we all knew. This pastor never modeled or championed groups personally. If you don't act like groups are a priority, then they never will be a priority. **If the leaders in your culture don't really behave like groups are important, then they won't be.** Simply put, your behavior has a way of reinforcing your belief.

I have been to that same "no-small-groups" church. The children's ministry environments are breathtaking. There is state-of-the-art technology at every entrance. Hallways and rooms are designed with jaw-dropping visuals that highlight the theme for each teaching series. They value excellence in everything they create. It is a church wonderland for any child.

There was only one problem. The ministry wasn't organized for children to interact with the same adult leaders every week. So each time kids showed up, they were ushered to tables with leaders who didn't really know them. Why? The lead pastor sent a clear message about what should be the priority. Since there were multiple times the church offered Sunday morning services, the pastor wanted the children's ministry to stay flexible. (Unfortunately, it seems that in some churches the primary role of children's ministry is to keep the kids busy so parents can go to church.) The pastor didn't want to create the expectation that families should come to the same hour every week. He was concerned if they got up late and missed their hour, they wouldn't come at all. So, it was important to him that every adult knew they could come to whichever hour they wanted. That one decision made it extremely difficult for kids to be connected to the same leader each week. It also created a pattern of behavior or a culture where small groups could never really work.

It communicated something else too. This philosophy suggested that what happened on the church's stage was more important than what happened in relationships. The church leaders behaved like drawing a crowd was more important than connecting in a circle. The children's ministry was just one example of how the church devalued small groups. Maybe that's part of the reason small groups never took off in their church. When small groups are not a priority everywhere, it's hard for them to be a priority anywhere. People are smarter than you think. No matter what you say you believe, people can tell what's important by the way you act. And your behavior will affect what they believe.

Maybe people decide small groups don't work because their church leaders don't act like they *believe* small groups really work.

Several years ago, a pastor asked me to meet with his elders and staff to help them evaluate their church. They had recently transitioned to a small group model and wanted to discuss ways to improve. After a few hours of talking through their strategy, one of the leaders asked this question: "What do you think is the best discipleship program for our Wednesday night gatherings?" Surprised by his question, I replied, "So you have a discipleship program at your church in the middle of the week?" He said, "Yes, we are just not sure that groups will really be the ultimate answer for discipleship." So I responded, "Then they probably never will be the answer." When he looked confused I explained, "As long as you have another answer, groups will probably never become *the* answer. If you want small groups to actually become the primary way you disciple people, then you need to start acting like you believe small groups are the best way to disciple people." You give energy to what you believe in most. And the people who follow your leadership are smart enough to know when you believe what you say.

It's simple. If you believe the best way to disciple people is to organize them into small groups, then act like it. When you create multiple options to disciple someone, you risk establishing competing systems that will ensure nothing works well. **Again, too many answers can guarantee nobody really knows the answer.** As long as you act like something else is really the answer then it probably will be.

BELIEF INFLUENCES BEHAVIOR AND BEHAVIOR INFLUENCES BELIEF. THEY ARE THE TWO MOST IMPORTANT CHARACTERISTICS TO UNDERSTAND WHEN YOU ARE TRYING TO SHAPE A CULTURE IN YOUR CHURCH.

HERE ARE TWO MORE TERMS YOU MAY WANT TO KNOW AS YOU READ THIS BOOK:

BELIEF:
The confidence or conviction that something is true.

BEHAVIOR:
A visible pattern of conduct that results from a particular belief.

If you are trying to create a culture where every kid has a place to belong, then there are three critical beliefs and behaviors you need to embrace.

BELIEF: The quality of relationships is linked to the quality of your structure.

BEHAVIOR: IMPROVE THE STRUCTURE.

BELIEF: The scope of your influence is determined by the success of your leaders.

BEHAVIOR: EMPOWER THE LEADER.

BELIEF: The truth of your message is amplified by the depth of your relationships.

BEHAVIOR: CREATE THE EXPERIENCE.

ONE

BELIEF
The quality of relationships is linked to the quality of your structure.
It might seem strange to put the words "structure" and "relationships" in the same sentence. They seem like unrelated topics, but we believe they are dependent on each other. Most people need some type of structure to help them connect consistently. Your potential to be successful in connecting people relationally is directly linked to how you organize your ministry. And when you actually start believing people need some type of organization to connect, then you will be more likely to practice the following behavior.

BEHAVIOR
IMPROVE THE STRUCTURE.
This means, you will spend time tweaking the systems in your organization to help people connect effectively. It suggests that someone on your staff will make leading a group strategy their focus. They will have to assume a variety of responsibilities that will include monitoring what *is* and *is not* working; arranging and re-arranging how people are organized in groups; and leveraging various platforms to lead people into small groups.

TWO

BELIEF

The scope of your influence is determined by the success of your leaders.

Every smart leader should embrace the idea that a ministry to kids or teenagers should never be built around one person. If you don't, you may promote a "pied piper" style of leadership that leads to a very unhealthy culture. It's possible you can become a barrier to discipleship if you decide you should be the one who disciples everyone. We hope that you, as a leader, are self-aware enough to know you have a limited capacity. If you expect to be successful at building a place where kids belong, then your smartest move is to help mobilize SGLs to do it.

BEHAVIOR

EMPOWER THE LEADER.

If you hope to give more kids a genuine sense of belonging, then you will need more leaders. Don't forget: you can't disciple kids in a crowd. Kids need to be in a context where they are known by someone if you hope to influence their faith. That's why you make recruiting, training, and developing leaders a priority. It's simple. If you want small group leaders to make a weekly investment in kids, then you need to make a weekly investment in small group leaders. So, start acting like what you do for leaders is just as important as what you do for kids.

THREE

BELIEF
The truth of your message is amplified by the depth of your relationships.
Here's the truth about truth. Kids tend to care more about what you say when they know you care about them. They are not compelled to embrace something simply because it's true. As far as they are concerned, it doesn't matter if it's true. It matters when it matters to them, and it matters to them even more when they know they matter to you. Does that mean it isn't important to teach or communicate truth? No. It just means you need to recognize that your message is best understood and received in the context of a caring relationship.

BEHAVIOR
CREATE THE EXPERIENCE.
This leads us back to the one thing you can ultimately do as a ministry leader: you can create an experience where kids have a better chance to connect with an SGL. Think about it. You can't make kids believe or force them to have deeper relationships. But you can create a place that makes it easier for them to belong and believe. That's why you have to work diligently on the weekly experience that is actually happening for the average kid. When it's all said and done, it's what happens in group that will determine your success.

So, let's summarize. If you believe the best way to disciple kids or teenagers is to connect them to consistent leaders, then you need to make sure you act like it. If you don't intentionally act like small groups matter, then people will probably never believe they matter. If you want to create a culture where small groups flourish then you need to have an ongoing plan for what happens with your structure, leaders, and experiences. If you are interested in having such a plan, then keep reading. That's what the rest of this book is about.

BEHAVIOR

IMPROVE THE STRUCTURE

BELIEF:

The quality of relationships is linked to the quality of your structure

IMPROVE THE STRUCTURE

Relationships don't just happen without . . .
an introduction.
an invitation.
a calendar.
a place to sit down.
some type of initiative on someone's part.

It takes a number of things working behind the scenes for relationships to happen. These things don't guarantee strong relationships, but they facilitate the possibility of people connecting. Before most relationships happen . . .
someone has to make the first move.
someone has to set a time.
someone has to start the conversation.
someone has to find a place to meet.

Relationships don't just happen.
They require some degree of initiative and intentionality.

Do you know why some small groups work and others don't?
We're going to make a suggestion that may seem counterintuitive.

Relationships need structure.

Now, before alarms go off in your head and you imagine a rigid routine to build better friendships, let's clarify. For some people, it seems strange to put the words *relationships* and *structure* in the same sentence. But a healthy amount of structure can fuel people so they can grow relationally.

HERE'S HOW WE DEFINE **STRUCTURE**:
HOW YOU ARRANGE OR MANAGE VARIOUS PARTS SO THEY CAN SUPPORT SOMETHING IMPORTANT.

So if we translate that for you as a ministry leader, we could ask the question this way:

How do you arrange or manage staff, volunteers, programs, budget, calendar, or even those who attend each week so everything supports a relational model?

Structure matters more than most leaders realize.

The right kind of structure can help things grow. Think about it . . .
what if a farmer only planted seeds randomly?
what if athletes only exercised when they felt like it?
what if a CEO rarely looked at the budget?
what it a pastor never prepared his sermon?

Okay, I know it might seem like that last one happens a lot.
But the point is without some intentional structure . . .
things don't grow the right way,
things usually don't move in a positive direction,
and things can't really improve.

Why are we quick to agree that structure helps most things grow, but somehow forget how much it matters in relationships?

Let's think about this. Most people assume we need structure for our faith to grow. Isn't that why . . .
God commanded us to take a day each week to recharge our faith?
Moses said to talk to your kids about their faith every morning and night?
Jesus suggested that we pray daily?
Your church probably plans a series on spiritual disciplines every year?

So, consider the question another way:
If structure can help you grow your business, your health, and your faith, why doesn't structure matter when you are trying to help people grow relationally?

If you really believe THE QUALITY OF YOUR RELATIONSHIPS IS LINKED TO THE QUALITY OF YOUR STRUCTURE, then you should try to **IMPROVE YOUR STRUCTURE** so relationships can thrive.

Have you ever considered that whatever tends to work in your church is working because you have improved your present structure to support it? You provide support to what you think is important.

Chances are . . .
You have a structure to support your Sunday morning services.
You have a structure to support global and local mission efforts.
You have a structure to support various education and ministry programs.
You even have a structure to support every kid who needs to poop.
But what kind of structure do you have to support the kind of relationships that will help people grow?

Your church should have systems in place to help people grow in their relationship with God and each other. You should be intentional about connecting people to people.

I (Reggie) read a blog by a pastor who had been critical of small groups. He believed that groups don't work for people, and that most people don't naturally grow in a group context. He argued that the significant relationships that had affected his spiritual formation had *just happened*. He even suggested that small groups were a westernized concept that had adversely affected the potential of people to experience authentic and biblical community.

The more I read, the clearer it became that much of his experience was a reaction to unhealthy small group models. He was disillusioned with a version of small groups that was unfocused, poorly led, and characterized by fill-in-the-blank Bible studies. It was also apparent that many of his descriptions referred to adult groups. But because I had respect for this leader, I honestly shared a sense of frustration with his negative experience with small groups.

Interestingly, after a few years he came back around as a believer in the idea that the right small group strategy can be a springboard for discipleship. That being said, there are few things I would like to state as disclaimers about building a structure that supports small groups.

No small group model is perfect
(unless you recruit perfect leaders and create a flawless organization).

All small groups are not created equal
(unless you are better at matching people than ChristianMingle.com).

Some people will need to go even smaller than small groups
(unless nobody in your group ever needs counseling or mentoring).

Small groups will need to be constantly tweaked
(unless you discover the secret formula that works for everyone, forever).

I hope there will always be smart critics around. (Of course, the world would be a lot better with fewer mean critics.) Our mission is too important to not ask hard questions so we can evaluate and improve what we do.

It seems that most leaders who are hyper-critical about small groups are frustrated by a system where the structure is either almost non-existent or far too rigid.

But after thirty-plus years of ministry, I still believe the most efficient way to connect kids and teenagers relationally is a healthy small group supported by the right kind of structure. At best, it paves the way for them to build a strong relationship with a leader who can personally disciple them. At a minimum, it gives them a place to belong and a consistent leader to nudge them in a positive direction in their faith.

If you want small groups to work in your ministry, you need to believe and behave like relationships don't just happen. Even if you can point to scenarios where relationships appeared to happen by chance, I suspect someone was still being intentional, something was still being arranged, and there was still a degree of structure. Whenever you have a handful of leaders who are drawn together by a strong desire to grow spiritually, there can be a kind of a relational magic. But it's rare, and not everyone will experience it.

For the rest of the world, where many people are not as . . .
extroverted,
or driven,
or committed,
or persuaded,
or believers,
or leaders,
there needs to be an alternative plan to encourage relational connections. Most relationships will not happen purely by accident. Many people still need a structure that makes it easier for them to find a place that is welcoming, safe, and sacred.

Be careful that you don't promote a version of church that is just for the few and the committed.

Local churches should aggressively confront the notion that discipleship is reserved for a certain breed of Christians who think exactly alike. If we don't challenge that mindset, those outside the walls of the church will never venture inside. Just remember: We are not called to disciple Christians who are trying to build community with other Christians. We are called to simply "make disciples." The early disciples didn't go into the world to find people who already believed so they could help them believe more deeply. They went on a rescue mission to find people who were not following Jesus so they could lead them to start following Jesus.

We think, as it relates to kids and teenagers, it's even more important to influence the structure they need to build relationships. Unless you . . .
assume kids will just figure out how to connect on their own,
believe that relationships don't need a prompt or a cue,
buy into the notion teenagers naturally move toward positive friendships,
simply believe you don't need a plan to help relationships grow,
you need to do something intentional.

Your church is surrounded by kids and teenagers who are guarded, isolated, skeptical, and vulnerable. If you are going to give them a place to belong, it will require extra effort on your part as a leader.

It's simple.

If you believe someone's faith is best developed through authentic community, then you should improve your structure so it supports relationships. Unless of course you think community just happens by accident—then your job is easy. Just sit back and wait. Don't do anything.

Most responsible leaders think relationships need a nudge or a prod and are trying to do something about it. We suggest that if you don't know exactly what to do, then start designing a structure that supports small groups. If you come up with a better idea, let us know. Until then, we would love for you to add your ideas to this conversation so we can improve how we create a culture where kids can belong.

ORGANIZE TO BE ORGANIC

(Let's talk about your **staff**.)

Hopefully you're not content to sit back and let relationships just happen. So, why don't you start improving your structure?

Get ready to do a little organizing and arranging.
Get ready to set a few rules.

Here's an idea. Go find the singularly most organized and inflexible person you know, and hire them to manage your small groups. Put them in charge of optimizing how your small groups will be arranged for everyone, forever. Make sure your Kindergartners understand the sacredness of their groups—preferably by having them sign a covenant committing to stay in their designated group for a pre-determined amount of time. After all, you want to make sure you give kids some stability.

Or, if that sounds too rigid, maybe you want to try something a little different. Even though we believe structure is essential for relationships, we probably all agree that too much structure can shut some relationships down.

Some people want to schedule their own calendar.
Some people don't want to be forced to share private thoughts.
Some people even like to have a say in who their friends are.

When I (Kristen) was 12, I asked to bring a friend on our family vacation. Traditionally, my family went to the beach with a family who had a little girl about the age of my younger sister. But that year I was more interested in listening to Tracy Byrd sing "Keeper of the Stars" while I got just-enough-burned on the beach than watching *Homeward Bound* and boogie boarding with the jellyfish. My mom's friend wasn't comfortable with me bringing a stranger, so she came up with a better plan. They would choose a friend for me. They knew someone my age who would be "just perfect."

If you've ever . . .
been set up on a date,
been randomly assigned college roommates,
or had your mom's friend choose your beach buddy,
then you probably know it's difficult to force relationships.

We've all been there. We know what it's like to try to manufacture a connection that feels disingenuous, artificial, or forced.

But there's a fine line between too much structure and not quite enough. A relationally driven model has to be supported with the right amount of structure. So, how do you know if you have enough structure? How do you know if you have too much?

There's not a magic formula. There's no set of rules to determine how much structure you need. But we can say this: your team will probably not agree about it. (This may come as a shock, since I'm sure you agree about everything else.) People are wired differently. Evidently, God has a sense of humor because He created a wide variety of people who have different outlooks when it comes to the amount of structure and order they prefer.

Some people plan vacations down to the minute,
while others prefer to decide each day as it comes.
Some people have a family calendar in a prominent place in their home,
while others haven't written a date on the calendar in their entire lives.

So, in this crazy world of differing opinions about how much structure is helpful for relationships to thrive, let's say this:

Relationships need structure, but structure isn't the goal.
The goal is relational connection.

Relationships need structure, but structure isn't the goal. The goal is relational connection.

The goal is for a kid to feel known by someone and to feel like they belong somewhere. If that is happening, chances are you have created the right amount of structure.

Still not clear? Maybe we can say it this way:

You may need to create a little more structure for your groups if . . .
kids can't name one person in their small group.
you aren't sure when or where groups are meeting.
SGLs are unclear about the purpose of a group.

You may have let structure get out of control when . . .
you've never allowed a kid to switch groups.
you dictate exactly when and where everyone meets.
SGLs are afraid of trying something new or deviating from your script.

When you organize to be organic, you create a structure that supports what's most important. You are inclined to implement a system of guiding principles rather than absolute rules. You delegate to SGLs who will adapt and change what needs to be changed in order to achieve the desired result, which brings us to one of the first things you should consider when it comes to structure.

. . . .

WHEN YOU ORGANIZE TO BE ORGANIC . . .
SOMEONE HAS TO OWN IT.

If groups are a priority in your ministry, someone needs to feel responsible for groups. You've probably already thought of that, but we wanted to make it really clear. It's actually why we wrote this book. You might consider the three behaviors and nine habits in this book as the job description for whoever is in charge of small groups.

First, you have to decide who will own it.

Maybe you own it—along with a whole bunch of other things.
Maybe you share these responsibilities with another staff member.
Maybe you hire someone specifically for this role.
Maybe you have a highly committed volunteer who owns it.

It's up to you to decide who owns it. But just remember, without focused, designated attention, groups will never work the way they should. In some ways, *small* actually takes *more* structure than large.

Nina Schmidgall leads the family ministry team at National Community Church in Washington, D.C. As a multi-site church, they started with a handful of small locations. When she talked about what led them to adopt a lead small emphasis, she said: "The thing that convinced us to be a lead small culture was growth. When we started, each of our locations had such a small number of kids that every campus *was* a small group. As our locations grew, we realized we were missing something. We wanted to put the emphasis back on relationships, and we knew we needed to structure things to get back there."

Something remarkable happened in Nina's ministry when it was small— *because* it was small. Relationships were helping kids grow an authentic faith. But as they grew larger, they had to get *more* intentional about structuring their ministry so they could keep relational connections strong.

Two Sides of a Ministry
Regardless of your church size, there are probably two components to your weekly ministry:

PROGRAMMING	GROUPS
What happens on the platform, or at the front of the room while people watch.	What happens in circles, or coffee houses, or bowling alleys while kids and teenagers participate.

When it comes to your staff, your hiring ratios for these two components aren't the same.

If you're just starting out or you are in a smaller church, maybe your hiring ratios are simple. It's just you. But you can apply this next principle to the percentage of attention, focus, or volunteers you designate to each component.

Quality production takes talented, focused people. But it takes roughly the same number of people to produce an event whether you have 50 or 500 in attendance. The same thing isn't true for groups. Just like you need more SGLs for 400 kids than you would for 20, you can't support 30 SGLs with the same number of staff that it took for only five. Your ratios are different. We will talk more specifically in the next section about the kind of attention your SGLs need. But for now let's just say, before you can even begin to give your groups the structure they need, someone has to own it.

WHEN YOU ORGANIZE TO BE ORGANIC . . .
AGE CHANGES THE RULES.

Remember the story about getting set up with a friend for the beach? That story may not make a lot of sense to someone who spends time working with toddlers and younger elementary kids. Why? Well, the postman could probably pick a playmate for a toddler with relative success. It might not be a friendship that takes off, but you stand a pretty good chance of making it work.

But if you work with older elementary, tweens, or teenagers, things are different. They have stronger opinions about who they hang out with and how they spend their time. Things change, and they want more independence and control over their world.

Here's a basic principle when it comes to improving the structure for kids:
The younger they are, the more structure they need.

Small groups for two and three-year-olds don't look the same as small groups for middle-schoolers. They are at very different stages, so the way you structure the groups should be different.

You might want to look at it this way . . .

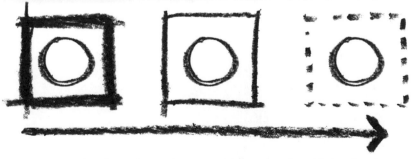

preschool – elementary – middle school – high school

When you oversee groups for younger kids, you need to exercise a higher level of control over things like time, place, snacks, and activities. As kids get older, your structure should provide enough flexibility for kids to determine how the group works best for them.

When I (Kristen) was leading a group of high school juniors several years ago, I remember watching another SGL do something I thought was remarkable. This particular leader had a group of seniors who had been together for four years. When the time came for our annual February retreat, her seniors were "so over it." They had been doing retreats like these since sixth grade, and there was a "been there, done that" mentality. Instead of launching into a campaign of shame to make sure her seniors knew their spiritual maturity was dependent on their attendance at this event, this leader went a different direction. She sought counsel from our church leadership, and they jointly decided to create a second option for her group. Her group spent the weekend of the retreat on a small group retreat of their own. The church gave that leader the same material they would be covering at the event, and the leader customized it for her seniors. They were able to cover the same topic, but on a level that was specific for them as almost-graduates.

What kind of impact do you think that weekend made on her group of seniors?

The older they are, the more flexible your structure should be.

Now, before you disagree and start writing a blog post about how student ministries need their seniors to be fully engaged so they can lead their peers, hold on. That's true. Juniors and seniors shouldn't be encouraged to check out of student ministry. There should be a small group structure in place that helps older kids thrive. When you improve your structure in the right way, there will be seniors who are committed not only to attending, but to plugging in to serve and lead in student ministry. But that won't be every senior. Some will be ready to move beyond what they have been doing for the past several years. So, if you lead a student ministry you should ask yourself this question: Does our structure have enough flexibility to maintain influence with those who are ready for something different?

If your only discipleship option for students (especially seniors) is for them to keep attending what they no longer want to attend, then maybe you should rethink your structure. You can't force students to come at a specific time or to a specific place any more than you can choose their best friend. You may need to become a little more organic—unless structure is the goal.

WHEN YOU ORGANIZE TO BE ORGANIC . . .
EVERYONE NEEDS A GOOD SEAT.

Your staff may never find a formula that ensures every kid will connect with their SGL and their group. But someone on your staff (the one who owns small groups) will constantly be placing kids in a group. They will be looking for ways to give kids a better group experience. They will do their best to give every kid a better seat.

A better seat will give a kid a better chance to . . .
see God.
connect with other believers.
grow in their faith.
meet their soul-mate.

Okay, maybe not that last one. But we do think where and how you place kids in groups has the potential to support group connection. Here are three priorities we think can help you give kids a better seat.

1. Fewer is Better
What are optimal small group ratios? We don't really know. But we asked dozens of smart leaders who have created and sustained a healthy lead small culture in their ministries, and here are the averages they gave us:

Preschool: 5-7

Elementary: 8-12

Middle School & High School: 8-12

Not every leader has the same relational capacity. Not every small group has the same level of consistency. Not every kid requires the same level of attention. For those reasons, you may never have a one-size-fits-all ratio for groups. But whenever you think about optimal group ratios, remember this: fewer is better. Then make adjustments based on a few other considerations:

When you think about your group ratios, consider *the attendance patterns of your audience*. For example, Kevin Ragsdale likes to place no more than 12 on a small group roll, so there will be an average of eight who show up weekly. As you make group placements, think about how often you expect kids to show up.

When you think about your group ratios, consider *the typical growth of a group*. Amy Fenton and Tom Shefchunas intentionally start groups smaller so they have room to grow throughout the year.

When you think about your group ratios, consider *what you're asking leaders to do*. If you encourage leaders to connect with every kid on their roster, regardless of whether or not they show up in the room, there will ultimately be a limit to how many kids you can assign to an SGL.

2. Common Interests Matter
In the months leading up to your promotion Sunday, the person in your ministry who owns small groups will have the task of placing kids in a group. That's a lot of responsibility. So, how will your ministry decide which kids go where?

After talking with leaders who have spent years placing kids in groups, the general consensus looks something like this:

If we had to unpack that a little more, we would say two things determine the way you will approach group placement.

THE SIZE OF YOUR MINISTRY
If you have a ministry of eight kids, it's simple. They all go in one group. But once your numbers start to grow, things get complicated. The larger your ministry, the more intentionality you will have to give to this question. The larger your ministry, the more layers you will need to add in order to place kids in groups.

THE AGE OF THE KIDS

The system you create for placing preschoolers will probably look different than the system you use for placing high-schoolers. For example, if you work with younger kids, gender may not be a factor when placing kids in group. Most leaders say they have mixed-gender small groups for kids until around third grade. Then they begin to separate guys' groups from girls' groups.

Remember, the older the kid, the more flexible the structure needs to be. That means staff who oversee older age groups will need more ways to filter groups so kids can connect.

STARTING WITH GROUPS IN MIND: KEVIN RAGSDALE
My goal in starting InsideOut (student ministry) was to one day split our ministry into middle school and high school. I also knew I wanted our small groups to be divided by gender, grade, school or geographic location, and friends, interests, hobbies, etc. That was the dream. When we started, however, there were only around 40 students sixth through twelfth grade showing up on a consistent basis. This caused us to look at our group structure in a completely different way. We followed the same guidelines, but we also adjusted groups based on the amount of students in each specific grade. In some cases, we put multiple grades together. We have always divided middle and high school students by gender regardless of the numbers. But early on we had sixth, seventh, eighth, and ninth grade guys together in one group, one tenth-grade guys' group, and one eleventh-and-twelfth-grade guys group. The same thing happened with our girls' groups. Again, this was based on how many students were showing up from a specific grade. As more students started attending, we began to divide the grades and then subdivide based on location and interests.

3. Guests Are Always Welcome

The good news is once you place every kid into a group, your job is done until next year. No one will move away. No one will come for the first time. Everyone will be happy with the group you selected for them, and you will never have to make an adjustment—unless of course you are working with real people instead of playing The Sims.

That's why there's an organic nature to group placement.

It's also why we don't think closed groups idea.

Sometimes we hear leaders advocate for a small group system where guests aren't welcome. Their arguments seem to be based on the idea that in order for kids to go "deeper" with their discipleship, they need to be surrounded by kids who are "as seasoned" in their faith. We think there's a false dichotomy between going deeper and being evangelistically driven. Sometimes including new kids in a group is exactly what that group needs in order to help kids move toward a more authentic faith.

When you give kids a closed group, you . . .
set them up to believe faith is only for insiders.
rob them of an opportunity to share their faith with others.
limit the questions that will be processed in the group context.

If guests are always welcome, you plan for them to show up. You create a system for assimilating them into group as smoothly as possible. Your system should be customized according to your church size and the age group of your kids. But if you're looking for ideas, here are a few specific ways other leaders handle assimilation.

"When new kids visit one of the NCC campuses, they simply join their age group. Our locations are small, so if we put all new or visiting kids together, they would be with kids of drastically different ages."
– **Nina Schmidgall** (All Ages)

"When we have a guest, I always ask the greeters to let them see if they know someone first. If they do, we let them visit that group. We know that seeing a familiar face will make them more comfortable."
– **Amy Fenton** (Elementary)

"When a student comes to InsideOut for the first time (and they are not with a friend), they go to a 'connect' group. In 'connect' students are invited to meet an engaging staff member to get an overview of what happens every week at InsideOut. The student fills out a survey to give us information about their interests. If they come back a second time, we have placed them in a group and have given their new leader their information. " – **Kevin Ragsdale** (High School)

"We have a 'special small group' for first time visitors. They go into this small group until the parent decides what service is a best fit for them." – **Jenny Zimmer** (Preschool)

No matter what system you create to assimilate new kids into small groups, you need some structure around it. You need someone on your staff to own it. And you may have to do some arranging and re-arranging if you want to give groups the right amount of structure so they can thrive. That's why you organize to be organic.

When you get in the habit of organizing to be organic,

what everyone does works together to make relationships win.

THINK STEPS, NOT PROGRAMS

(Let's talk about your **programs**.)

When I (Reggie) first started working as a student pastor, I thought my goal was to create as many effective programs as possible for teenagers.

It seemed logical.

More programs meant more opportunities to keep teenagers out of trouble.
More programs meant more options to reach a variety of students.
More programs meant more volunteers investing in teenagers.
More programs meant more students learning truth.

Oh and if I'm really honest, more programs meant I looked more successful as a leader.

I had a host of programs that were somewhat successful. That is, if you measure success by how many participate, or the number of compliments you get from leaders or parents. But I wish someone had explained to me in my first decade of ministry what I learned in the last two decades. It's important to clarify the primary win in your ministry before you can evaluate if a specific program is successful.

When you think about the programs in your ministry, here is a strategic question to ask:
"Did the program help you move people in the direction you want them to go?"

Of course, that implies you know where you want them to go. Remember, we think the win for your ministry is connecting kids in a healthy small group. If you agree, you evaluate the programs in your ministry to see if they are helping or hindering small groups.

Some programs in your ministry may be working so well they are hindering something more important from working.

Here's a sobering possibility:
Some programs in your ministry may be working so well they are
hindering something more important from working.

As long as you have limited facilities, volunteers, budget, calendar, and
energy, you have to prioritize those resources around what you think is
most important. If you want small groups to win, you need to take a hard
look at the rest of what you do.

One of three things will be true about your programs.
- They are moving kids away from small groups.
- They are moving kids toward small groups.
- They are not moving kids anywhere.

In the early days of North Point Community Church, a few leaders
approached us about implementing a program for new moms. It seemed
like an easy win. These were seasoned and responsible leaders (who
promised they would do all of the work). They had enormous influence
and passion for this ministry. They also had the resources of a reputable
national organization behind the program they wanted to start. And since
the program was designed to build a bridge to families who were outside
the church, it was easy for us to say "yes." Within a few years the program
was extremely successful.

Then, during one of our annual retreats with our ministry directors, I asked
a simple question. "Are there any programs we do that are not helping us
move people where we want them to go?" My heart sank when one of our
directors named this program because I knew the battle we would fight
with key leaders if we discontinued it. But we immediately knew she was
right. This program had become so popular, it had tapped more and more
of our best volunteers. It consistently demanded extra facilities, technical
support, and budget with every passing season. Our staff had become
inundated with problem solving and managing numerous details related to
the needs of this program. But all of that was secondary to the realization
that this program was not strategic in moving people toward groups or
deeper relationships. So, we made the hard decision to discontinue.

Of course, when we explained our reasoning to the program leaders, they
kindly agreed it was the right decision.

That is, after numerous phone calls to the elders and executive staff,
a heated petition, and a passionate phone call from the national

organization's president. It was a painful and agonizing process. But our team was confident it was the right thing to do, because the program had become a competing system that was hindering what we wanted to happen relationally with families. I'm not going to tell you the name of the organization. The good news is they have recently re-invented their program so it's more strategic.

Just remember this:
Sometimes you have to stop doing something that works if you want something more important to work better.

From time to time you have to re-evaluate everything you do if you want to gain new momentum in the critical areas of your ministry. One of the keys to building an effective ministry is distinguishing between random programs and strategic programs.

Random programs are created to meet various needs.
Strategic programs are created to lead people to what's next.

Random programs work independently.
Strategic programs work together.

Random programs tend to establish competing systems.
Strategic programs establish complementary systems.

Random programs function as activities.
Strategic programs function as steps.

In *The 7 Practices of Effective Ministry*, Andy Stanley, Lane Jones and I (Reggie) introduce the practice of "Think Steps, Not Programs." In the book, we explain the importance of evaluating programs to see if they are working as steps to move people relationally in the right direction. We say a program that is working like a step should be easy, clear, and strategic.

PROGRAMS SHOULD MAKE IT *EASY*,	PROGRAMS SHOULD BE PROMOTED IN A *CLEAR* WAY	PROGRAMS SHOULD BE *STRATEGIC* IN THE WAY
not hard, for people to participate and move to what is next.	so people can actually see how and why they are important.	they support the primary goal or priority of the ministry.

As you create a lead small culture for kids and teenagers, it's important to rethink the various programs in your ministry so they can function as steps to the small group experience.

WHEN YOU THINK STEPS, NOT PROGRAMS . . .
PLATFORMS ENHANCE SMALL GROUPS.

Every program has a platform that can be leveraged to influence people to value groups. If you want parents, kids, and teenagers to believe small group is important, then what you say about small groups on every platform is important.

Casting Vision
I'm sure most people are such fans of what you do they heard your vision once and are now raving fans forever. But the rest of the crowd is actually going to leave your church this week and do their normal routine of wakeboarding, cave spelunking, or watching the latest Marvel superheroes movie. In their case, you may need to look for creative ways to keep them thinking about the value of small group. Just remember: It's the nature of a vision to leak. So they may need to hear it again, and again, and again in as many creative ways as possible if you want them to make groups a consistent priority.

The value of small groups can be communicated by . . .
a story in the pastor's sermon.
a video before a program starts.
a clever, funny announcement.
an interview with a small group leader.

All of these things can help parents understand your strategy a little better, too. They can explain why parents should commit to attending the same hour every week, or why kids are getting a random postcard in the mail from another adult, or why their second-grade daughter dressed in pajamas to go to church.

Part of the success of every program should be linked to how well it elevates the idea of finding authentic community. Program directors should consider asking and answering the question, "What can we say or do to help people know what's next?" Whenever there is reluctance or resistance to championing small groups from a platform, it may be an indicator that a program is out of sync or no longer strategic.

Managing Time

Nothing communicates the value of the small group or a small group leader any more than how you structure time. If a speaker goes forty minutes and small group lasts ten, it suggests what's happening on the platform is at least four times more important than what is happening in small group. (It may also suggest someone doesn't understand the attention span of a four-year-old boy).

By the way, cheating your small group leaders out of time with their group is also a great way to get rid of your best SGLs. Smart leaders can tell what matters most by how you arrange the segments in your program. Our surveys indicate an average small group should get about 30 minutes of interaction each week in your programming. Their time together may happen at multiple points in the overall experience. For example, in the elementary ages you may open with a ten-minute small group activity at the beginning of the hour and end with fifteen to twenty minutes of more focused small group time later. Your goal is to create a structure that guards the small group time so it becomes the priority within the program.

> "We try to give about 30 minutes for the average small group. It's also why we do our student groups on Sunday night. That way there is really no time limit on the back end if they are having great discussion. They can even carry the conversation into dinner."
> — **Kevin Ragsdale** (High School)

WHEN YOU THINK STEPS, NOT PROGRAMS . . .
EVENTS SOLIDIFY SMALL GROUPS.

Those of us who have worked in student ministry are convinced long bus rides lead to stronger small groups.

Okay, so there is no statistical information to back this up.
But, we think an eight-hour bus ride to a student camp gives a small group leader more credibility in a student's life than at least 20 Sundays. If the bus happens to break down, it probably equals another three months of Sundays in bonding time.

Maybe that's why many churches who are building a lead small culture rethink how they design and position events (or bus rides) to make small groups win.

"All of our events are groups-based or we don't do them. Groups, not individuals, are assigned to cabins, buses, lunchtimes, etc. We plan our talks for camp by figuring out what we want to happen in groups first. The program then becomes set-up for group. We ask leaders to come with their kids to camp, not help us run camp. The plan is for them to have experiences together as much as possible. "
– **Tom Shefchunas** (Middle School)

"Our trips and experiences are built with small groups in mind. For example, it's more important to ask, 'How many small groups will be on this trip?' than it is to ask, 'How many students are coming?' I would rather have empty beds in cabins if we have to. Prioritizing for small groups is more important than renting one less room."
– **Darren Kizer** (All Ages)

Rethinking Camps
I (Reggie) have worked as a speaker and leader at camps for over 30 years. Most of my summers have been spent training student pastors and small group leaders. After years of wrestling with what makes a camp experience work, I have become more determined than ever to help leaders rethink how they do camps. The optimal camp experience happens when the leaders who produce the camp and the churches who bring students both have a shared value related to small groups. Too many camps function more like random events than strategic experiences. Every camp should be designed to have lasting value for the church beyond the week of camp.

A few years ago I sat down with a host of student pastors, including Ben Crawshaw and Kevin Ragsdale, to analyze the camp experience. We dreamed about creating a unique student camp built around the value of small groups.

We came up with ten characteristics that make a student camp small group friendly.

1. Small group leaders, not random adult chaperones, attend with students.
2. Main sessions are limited in production and time to complement group.
3. Resources are provided during camp to enhance the small group experience.
4. SGLs are valued and trained during the camp experience.
5. Each camp is built around age group focus for relevance.
6. Speakers are coached so messages set up small group time.
7. Activities or mission opportunities are organized around small groups.
8. Churches are provided with a follow-up curriculum for small groups after camp.
9. A targeted social media strategy is designed to engage parents with camp.
10. Logistics are organized so small group leaders can stay focused on relationships.

Too many camps focus their energy on creating a "wow factor" for the main stage sessions while neglecting to make small groups a priority. Both can happen, but unless the camp leadership authentically values small groups, the production will be the priority. There is a trend at many camps to over-produce and wear kids out physically and emotionally so there is not a lot of energy left to connect in the context of a group.

Those who create camp experiences should take a fresh approach. They should act like what happens in the small group is more important than what happens on the stage.

Think about it this way:
Camp typically lasts a week.
Speakers and worship leaders leave.
Students go back to their church with their small group leaders.
Which relationships do you think are most important?

Making Events Strategic
The same logic we apply to camp should be applied to every event. When you create a lead small culture, you tend to look at every event through a new lens. You realize events have incredible potential to solidify the relationships in groups.

Now, you may be asking, "What about kids who are visiting, new, or are not yet in a small group?"

A strategic event can actually be one of the best ways to help new kids get connected deeper and faster. Instead of hanging out with a random chaperone who they may never see again, a small group focused event will connect kids with SGLs and peers they will see again if they show up to your weekly experience.

"We are in the process of launching a Saturday event where small group leaders and kids can spend time together outside of church. We also leverage events like Camp KidJam by encouraging small group leaders to attend with their kids to help deepen the relationship."
– **Adam Duckworth** (Elementary)

Serving Together as Groups

If you've ever taken a group on a mission trip or service project, you know the value these experiences have when it comes to deepening relationships. Time spent taking care of the homeless, working with disadvantaged kids, or becoming actively involved helping a different people group creates a unique sense of teamwork and mission. It's also a great training ground for SGLs and their few to develop ministry skills. When small groups serve together, they can discover something they may not experience through Bible study, prayer, and worship.

WHEN YOU THINK STEPS, NOT PROGRAMS . . .
VOLUNTEERS REINFORCE SMALL GROUPS.

Making small groups win is a team sport. Just like your staff structure should support small groups, all other volunteer teams exist to support groups. Let's make a list of some of the non-SGL volunteers you might have for your weekly experience:

Hallway greeters	Crowd control
Room greeters	Band and worship teams
Large group hosts	Food teams
Large group presenters/speakers	Security
Production and tech teams	Registration teams
Actors for dramas	The guy you test your games on

You have a variety of volunteers who have very different jobs. It's easy for everyone to be so hyper-focused on what they do that they miss the bigger picture. That's why it's important to clarify the primary win. When the primary win is defined in terms of an effective small group experience, it will synchronize your volunteer teams so they can work together. When everyone on the team clearly understands the goal, it changes how they do what they do. Let's use a typical high school program to illustrate this principle.

Say you define the primary win for your student ministry as follows:

"We win when students have meaningful interactions during group that influence their faith in Jesus and deepen their relationships with others."

Now, imagine if you wrote that win on a board and invited all of your volunteers into the room. After a short explanation of why it's important to give kids a place to belong, you explain the win to everyone. You say something like:

If you are a HOST on stage, we need you to use transitional statements and champion group from the platform. Your win happens when you inspire and motivate students to make their small group meaningful.

If you are a WORSHIP LEADER, we need you to create an environment that breaks down walls and prepares students to be open to hear the message. Your win happens when students are moved to participate together in collective worship.

If you are the SPEAKER, we need you to position the message to set up small group. Your win happens when what you say becomes a springboard for dynamic and meaningful conversation during group.

If you are COOKING hamburgers, we need you to know you are not just cooking hamburgers; you are providing an informal time for groups to connect. Your win happens when students hang around longer after group and go a little deeper in their relationships.

If the message, music, and food are incredible, but kids don't connect in small group, the program wasn't a step.

WHEN YOU THINK STEPS, NOT PROGRAMS . . .
RESOURCES SUPPORT SMALL GROUPS.

If you act like you believe small groups are important, then you may need to spend your budget like you believe it. There are a number of resource indicators that small groups are really a priority in your church.
How you . . .
build and design your facilities.
pay the staff that directs small group ministry.
invest to develop SGLs.
allocate your budget to help small groups activities.

Reallocating Budget
As my (Elle's) church transitioned to a lead small culture, we spent time reviewing our budget in light of our priority on groups. Years ago, we spent around 25 percent of our annual budget on monthly events and designated very little toward supporting small groups. But because we were going to begin making some bigger asks of our leaders, we wanted to use our budget to support those asks. That's why we actually cut our scheduled events in half and reallocated money from our events budget to support groups. Now, we can reimburse leaders when they host a small group party of their own, give leaders thank-you cards and gift certificates when we see them doing a great job, and provide child care for a leader so they can lead. Our small group budget dollars are spent in ways that have less of a "wow" factor—but we believe they are making a bigger impact.

Evaluating Programs
So let's recap.

The programs in your church should function as steps. But chances are . . .
some programs are not moving people where they need to go.
some programs are just repeating what you're doing somewhere else.
some programs are creating competing systems.
some programs require too much energy for what they actually accomplish.

Why don't you make a list of all the programs in your ministry?

- Circle the programs you can change to be more strategic.
  (Make a specific list of improvements to make them work better.)
- Put an "x" by the programs you should consider killing.
  (Maybe write down a date when you want to bury them. It could make you feel better.)
- Underline the programs that are most strategic.
- Make an additional list of any programs you think you should add.

In all of these cases, you either need to stop something or change something; you can't afford to leave things the way they are.

Several years ago I (Reggie) was eating dinner with a marketing executive from Nike. He informed me that Steve Jobs had just visited their headquarters and made an intriguing remark that had them rethinking everything.

Jobs had said, "You guys make some incredible products. But you also make a lot of crap. Why don't you just stop making the crap?"

I'm sure your church does some amazing things. But maybe you have some programs that aren't so amazing or strategic. Why don't you stop doing what's less strategic, and do more of what really works? Create programs that work as steps toward relationships.

When you get in the habit of thinking steps, not programs, kids are more likely to end up where you want them to be.

MOVE TO
THE RHYTHM

(Let's talk about your **calendar**.)

Life has a rhythm.

Your life has a rhythm.

You probably brush your teeth before going to bed.
Maybe you get up around the same hour every morning.
You might even shop at the same grocery store when you need some
Double Stuf Oreos.

There's something about having a rhythm to your life that makes it more
comfortable and efficient. Some things move almost automatically, below
the surface, unnoticed. But if you think about it, there's something about
the rhythms of your life that reflect what you value.
If you brush your teeth, you probably value hygiene.
If you wake up in the morning, maybe it's because you value work.
If you shop for Double Stuf Oreos, well, we're not sure what that reveals.
But you get the point.

What you do in the everyday patterns of life demonstrates what you value.
And when you do something repeatedly, it can actually make you value it more.

Maybe that's why when Moses stood on the edge of Canaan and spoke to
the nation of Israel about passing on faith to future generations, he said this:

*"These commandments that I give you today are to be on your hearts.
Impress them on your children. Talk about them when you sit at home and
when you walk along the road, when you lie down and when you get up.
Tie them as symbols on your hands and bind them on your foreheads.
Write them on the doorframes of your houses and on your gates."*
Deuteronomy 6:6-9

Moses was doing something rather brilliant. He was anchoring the faith of the Israelite people to the natural rhythms of life. If we were to paraphrase Moses' message, it would go something like this: "If you are going to make these truths stick in the hearts of kids, you will have to be more deliberate about moving to the rhythm. In the future, there will be things that distract you. But if you make faith a part of the rhythm of your life, it will be a priority for you and for the generations to come."

The Israelites who listened to Moses that day understood something about having God in the rhythm of life. As they wandered in the desert, they ate manna every morning. They followed a cloud of smoke during the day and a pillar of fire at night. But in Canaan, it would be harder to remember. Moses, like a good leader, looked into the future. In a land flowing with milk and honey, he knew they would no longer be dependent on manna. The rhythm of their lives was changing, and he knew they would have to be more deliberate about keeping God in the day-to-day moments.

Moses knew something we think is essential for you to remember as you improve your structure to create a lead small culture.

When you make faith a part of the rhythms of life, it becomes more fluid, more natural, and more everyday.

That's why we encourage every SGL to . . .
invite themselves over for a nightly dinner in the home of their second graders.
show up to tuck in their four-year-olds at night.
surprise their middle schoolers (and family) by cooking breakfast on a Saturday morning.

Never mind. That could get a little weird. Actually, that's why we think it's so important for your ministry—and your SGLs—to partner with families.

We think two things are true:
No one will influence a kid more than a parent.
A parent isn't the only influence a kid needs.

If you want to have a significant impact in the life of a kid, you should influence two types of people: parents and small group leaders. Of course kids will have other adult influences in their life—and that's a good thing. But when you can influence parents and SGLs who are a part of a kid's "everyday" rhythm of life, you stand a better chance of giving them an "everyday" kind of faith.

The best way to leverage parents and SGLs is to synchronize their efforts. We say it all the time: Two combined influences have a greater impact than just two influences. When you get SGLs and parents on the same page, you significantly increase your influence in a kid's life. That's the power of synergy. It's the magic of repetition. Children learn best through routine. So, when families and SGLs move to the same rhythm, it helps accentuate learning and development.

The more people in a kid's life who are moving to the same rhythm, the greater the impact. The more you cooperate with the way life naturally happens, the more integrated faith will become.

Moses recognized the danger of a compartmentalized faith. He anticipated the people's tendency to segment God into an isolated category instead of viewing Him as the integrating force that influences all of life. It's characteristic of humans to create an image of God that is so narrowly defined it separates Him completely from culture. Instead of seeing everything as connected to God's story, we love to categorize and segment our faith.

But notice Moses never said, "For the sake of our faith, maybe we should stay isolated in the wilderness. Our faith is safer here." Instead, he pushed ahead to invade Canaan with a plan. What he handed the Israelites that day was a strategy to create a rhythm that would help keep their faith alive. It was a rhythm that would break down the walls of every culture to reveal a God whose story transcends time and space.

And it was effective. Years later, the Psalmist recorded something remarkable.

"He (the LORD) decreed statutes for Jacob and established the law in Israel, which he commanded our ancestors to teach their children, so the next generation would know them, even the children yet to be born, and they in turn would tell their children. Then they would put their trust in God and would not forget his deeds but would keep his commands."
Psalm 78:5-7

Generations later, after the conquest of Canaan, after the period of the Judges, after the rise of the monarchy, the Israelites had a faith that was anchored to the God who led them through the wilderness. They still told

The more people in a kid's life who are moving to the same rhythm, the greater the impact.

the stories. They wrote it out in Psalms. Why? Because they had the kind of everyday faith that stands the test of time.

When faith is something that only happens in church, it doesn't integrate into everyday life, and it fades. We've heard all the arguments for why the church should resist culture and know there is something about following Jesus that will change the way you live. Sure, your life will look different from the life of an unbeliever. But that doesn't mean you move to an entirely different rhythm. As a general rule, you shouldn't make culture your enemy.

That is, as long as . . .
you speak with language,
you play music,
you use air conditioning,
and kids wear clothes to church,
you will always do ministry within the context of culture.

But if you're smart, you can leverage the natural rhythms of culture to give kids an everyday faith. You can move to the rhythm that parents and SGLs are already programmed to move to. You can create a ministry that cooperates with the rhythm of the everyday.
It works with the seasons of the year.
It adjusts to the seasons of a kid's life.
It cooperates with the seasons of relationships.

The rhythm of your ministry is a structure issue. The way you organize your calendar and the way you leverage your time has the potential to support critical relationships. So, create a structure for your small groups that moves to the rhythm.

SMALL GROUPS SHOULD MOVE TO THE RHYTHM BY . . .
COOPERATING WITH THE PATTERNS OF THE TYPICAL YEAR.

There are natural rhythms to a year. The seasons come and go—or if you live in Muleshoe, Texas, the season just comes, and it stays. There's a time to reap, a time to sow, and a time to board up your windows if you live in Florida in early September.

If you are creating a ministry that moves to the rhythm in order to give kids an everyday faith, you need to consider the natural rhythms of the year.

The calendar has a rhythm.
Regardless of your theology about holidays, the kids and parents and SGLs in your community care about

Valentine's Day	Halloween
St. Patrick's Day	Thanksgiving
Easter	Christmas
Labor Day	New School-Year's Eve

That doesn't mean you have to create a program for every holiday, but it does mean you should think about them. Every holiday has a feel to it. Have you ever wondered why storefronts change their window displays or why sitcoms will have a "Valentine" episode or why Starbucks doesn't offer their best-selling pumpkin spice latte year-round? They are tapping into the rhythm of the year. They are leveraging the calendar.

So, here's a question. How do you leverage the calendar year to strengthen group?

....

Think scope and cycle
A few years ago, we coined the phrase "scope and cycle" as a way to talk about the rhythm of our messaging for kids and students.

Scope	Cycle
A comprehensive plan that prioritizes what you teach	Your plan to re-visit and reinforce what you teach so it's effective

....

Some educators use the term "sequence" instead of "cycle." But sequential learning is more effective with concepts that build in a linear fashion. First you learn to count, then you learn addition, then multiplication, then pre-algebra, then quantum physics. Once you master a concept, then you are ready to move on to something more complex.

Thinking in terms of sequential learning can be misleading when it comes to faith development unless you . . .
learn everything you need to know the first time.
immediately and forever apply every sermon after you hear it.
never discover something new in a passage of scripture you've heard or read before.

When you think in terms of cyclical learning, you recognize core truths will have fresh meaning with every new life stage. Your scope prioritizes what you will teach, and your cycle strategically recycles those principles again and again. There's something about repeating what matters that helps it stick. So, as you move to the rhythm of the year, your core message should be repeated in moments when it can connect most. If you are going to talk to preschoolers about how God made the world, why not do it in the spring when the school is talking about Earth Day and their parents are taking them to the park? If you are going to talk to elementary kids about having respect for authority, why not do it at the beginning of the school year when they are introduced to new authority figures who will be with them every day? If you are going to talk to teenagers about moral purity, why not do it in February or March before Spring Break, prom, and swimsuit season?

When you leverage the rhythm of the calendar, you partner with parents and small group leaders because you communicate a message that works with the natural rhythm of life.

Your community has a rhythm.
While some holidays and seasons are universal, some patterns in the year are unique to your specific community. Whether it's the Pecos, Texas, rodeo in June, the Memphis, Tennessee, music festival in May, or the Chandler, Arizona, ostrich festival in March, you probably have some community events that are a part of the rhythm of your year.

You can either intentionally align your calendar to move with the rhythm of your community, or you can ignore it. But if you ignore the rhythm of your community, you will have a hard time aligning parents and SGLs because—guess what?—they live in your community.

So, when it's hockey season, or the fair comes to town, or *American Idol* decides to host auditions right in your backyard, use it. Embrace it. Leverage it.

Also, sometimes the best way to embrace the rhythms of your community is to take a break.

"We have chosen to not do student programming on Spring Break, Easter, Mothers' Day, Memorial Day, Labor Day, and two weeks at Christmas."
– **Kevin Ragsdale** (High School)

If you've read that list and now suspect Kevin is a heretic, don't worry. It's not because Kevin hates those holidays or what they represent. Actually, Kevin is saying that he wants his small groups to cooperate with the home. That means when there's a significant event that can be leveraged best by a parent, he doesn't want to compete. His groups move to a rhythm that complements what happens at home.

Your ministry has a rhythm.
The rest of your community might not be aware, but you probably have some rhythms that have become part of your church culture. Maybe it's a summer camp, a giving campaign, a church-wide emphasis on service, a family experience, a Christmas program, or an annual chili cook-off. Whatever rhythms are a part of your church calendar, you can and should evaluate how they work to support groups.

"Our student ministry takes students on mission teams in June, so in July our elementary programming is staffed largely by our students who have just returned from their trips. They are excited and we take advantage of that, showing them that there is a mission field in their own church with the elementary kids. They do a tremendous job and many of them will plug in and serve in the fall." – **Bobbi Miller** (Elementary)

One of the most significant rhythms of your ministry may be your trends in attendance. If you are like most of the ministries we talk to, your attendance patterns look something like this:

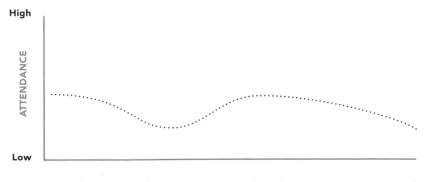

Aug - Sep - Oct - Nov - Dec - Jan - Feb - Mar - Apr - May - Jun - Jul

Your patterns may look different, but the point is the same. You should move to the rhythm of your ministry attendance patterns. How are you scheduling so groups can make the most of high attendance seasons? How are you anticipating low attendance months and planning accordingly?

SUMMERTIME

Let's talk about the summer. Most staff who work with small group ministries have some opinions about what to do with the summer. It's low attendance. Families go on vacation. SGLs go on vacation. It's sunny outside, and people just don't want to spend the morning inside. So, do your small groups continue to meet?

We don't have an answer for you. You will have to decide. What we can say is this: many children's ministries make a decision to use video-driven curriculum in order to give their production teams some time off. Some also discontinue small groups in order to let their leaders have more time with their own families. In most middle school and high school ministries though, the summer is a critical time for small groups to strengthen their connection. Students need leaders who can go to camp with them and make the most of their summer vacation.

However you decide to structure your groups, just remember they should complement, and not compete, with the attendance patterns in your ministry. When you cooperate with the rhythms of the year, you align parents and SGLs to incorporate faith into everyday life.

SMALL GROUPS SHOULD MOVE TO THE RHYTHM BY . . .
CONSIDERING THE LIFECYCLE OF THE AVERAGE GROUP.

Just like every Tupperware-enclosed leftover in your ministry fridge, every group has a lifecycle.

When you're improving a structure that supports groups, it's important to consider how groups change. Each phase of a group presents unique opportunities and challenges. And when you understand what those are, you can move to the rhythm of the group.

Every group has a beginning.
The beginning of a group, like the beginning of a new friendship, is full of discovery. It can be exciting. It can also make some people a little

uncomfortable. When you consider the lifecycle of your groups, you know what happens during the first group experiences matters more. Kids are getting a first impression of each other and of their leader. So, ask yourself this question: What can our ministry do to facilitate positive introductions during the first weeks of a group's time together?

Here's a basic principle to consider: The older the kid, the longer it will take for SGLs to build credibility and small groups to establish a connection. A preschooler trusts their SGL simply because they're a big person. As kids get older, SGLs have to earn their trust. So, as you build your scope and cycle, you might not want to have your middle school sex talk three weeks into a new year.

Some groups change in the middle of the year.
Every group has a unique story. There may be times an SGL moves away, a group loses momentum, or a group grows so fast you have to find a way to divide. When a group goes through a mid-cycle transition, whatever it is, there are a few things you can do to help make the transition smooth.

1. **Plan for it.** If the kids in your groups only know one adult, it will be hard for them to transition to someone else. Whether it's a coach, an apprentice, or the greeters in your hallways, who are you strategically positioning to take a group if an SGL leaves or a group divides?

2. **Over-communicate.** If the parents in your ministry have caught your vision for groups, they will care when a group changes. It's important to let parents know as early as possible. Don't let their kid be the first one to communicate when a change has happened. You move first, and give them time to ask questions.

3. **Move slowly when possible.** When a group grows, and grows, and grows, you will eventually have to make a decision to divide the group. If you want every kid to be known, they can't stay in a group of thirty. That's not a small group. If you haven't already done so, introduce a new SGL to co-lead the group. Give the group time to connect. Let the two SGLs work with you to divide the list of kids and come up with a plan for their transition. Let the leaders spend a few weeks connecting with the kids who will be on their list—*just to connect*. Then make an announcement to the group.

4. **Consider the season.** If you *know* you are going to ask a leader to leave, it's better to do it before student camp than after. If you *know* a group needs to divide, it's better to split them in January than right at Christmas. Whenever you make a change, consider the rhythm of a year and the season of the group so you can select a time that works.

5. **Stay positive.** Change is hard. When groups encounter change mid-cycle, you will probably encounter pushback from parents, or kids, or both. You can and should listen to their concerns. But stay positive. Sometimes change is the best thing for a group.

Every group has an end.
As much as we think consistency is essential for a healthy lead small culture, we think kids *should* have more than one small group experience as they move through various age group ministries. It's not that group relationships formed in preschool won't last beyond kindergarten, but small groups shouldn't. No SGL should stay with a group from birth to graduation—that's one reason kids have parents. There are seasons for kids and seasons for groups.

Actually, research shows that kids who have five or more adults who invest in their faith over time have a greater chance of having a mobilized faith. So, when you create a lead small culture, you give kids someone—again and again. You give them multiple adults as they move through your family ministry from birth through graduation because you anchor their personal faith to a community of faith.

As a group ends, remember that you are helping kids and families move from one life-stage to another as smoothly as possible. Here's one important principle: The older the kid, the longer the transition will take. This is especially true when you are transitioning someone from one age group ministry to the next.

Four-year-olds into Kindergarten – one month
Fifth grade into middle school ministry – two months
Eighth grade into high school ministry – three months
Seniors into whatever comes next – one year

TRANSITIONING SENIORS
Several years ago, I (Kristen) led a group of senior girls. As May drew near, I remember having mixed emotions. Even though the church celebrated

our group with a graduation dinner and handed me a gift card as a sign of gratitude for the past four years, I couldn't help but feel that my time with this group was incomplete. It felt like I was letting go, just when they were leaning in.

After talking with the youth minister at my church, I decided to commit to an extra year with my group. My goal was simple. I didn't want to let go until they were connected to someone else. I knew graduation was a critical transition, and I didn't want them to navigate it alone.

Some of the girls were planning to live at home and get a job after graduation. Some went to local state universities, and others moved away to universities around the country. Their first semester, I visited each of the college campuses that was within driving distance; I went on a weekend so we could attend a church near their campus together. I set up a day each week to send messages on Facebook (since that's where they connected best at the time). When the girls were home for holidays, I planned a Christmas party and sleepover.

A lot of what I did that year was both systematic and organic. Each girl experienced transition in her own unique way, so the amount of time I spent with each individual wasn't equal. But for most, our relationship went deeper in that one year than it had in the four years prior. The challenges they faced were more significant. The decisions they had to make held greater weight. By the end of that year, I was more convinced than ever that graduates need more than a Sunday celebration to transition into the next stage of life.

Now I remind church leaders every time I get the chance that high school graduation should not be viewed as a finish line, but another critical transition. Remember this:

DON'T DISCONNECT WHEN THE STAKES ARE THE HIGHEST. INSTEAD, TAP INTO YOUR RELATIONAL INFLUENCE WHEN THE FELT NEED IS THE GREATEST.

Whether you are transitioning seniors to college, fifth graders to middle school, or four-year-olds to Kindergarten, transitioning effectively takes time.

It also takes connection. Remember, if you are creating a culture where parents and SGLs work together to impact the "everyday" faith of a kid, you have to get them on the same page. Transitions give you a unique opportunity to get your parents and SGLs together—in the same room—to share something that will help them navigate the year ahead with success.

Think about it this way. Whenever a kid transitions, you can do two things: Give parents and leaders helpful information related to their kid's stage of life. Connect parents with SGLs so they know they have someone on their team.

When you align parents and SGLs, you mobilize two influences to have a greater combined impact in the life of a kid. If you want to fight for everyday, authentic faith in the next generation, you need to support the relationships that matter most. You need to move to the rhythm.

 When you get in the habit of moving to the rhythm, you cooperate with what is already happening so groups happen better.

BEHAVIOR

EMPOWER THE LEADER

BELIEF:

The scope of your influence
is determined by the success of
your leaders

EMPOWER THE LEADER

It's just a wild guess.
Maybe we've got you all wrong.
But we think maybe . . . just *maybe* . . .

You got into ministry because you care about kids.
You believe kids are capable of really big things.
You want kids to know and love God.
And you probably even like spending time with them. (You know, most of the time.)

And since you care about kids, and you know the best way to help a kid know God is to give them someone who knows God, maybe you went into ministry because you thought that person could be you.

But here's the thing. *That person can't be you.*

At least, you can't be that person for every kid. Your capacity is limited.

The average person has a relational capacity of about five to eight people. That means if there are more than eight kids in your ministry, you've already reached your relational capacity. You're already in over

your head. Once you've surpassed your relational capacity, you can no longer . . .
know every name.
remember every birthday.
follow every story.
partner with every parent.
disciple every kid.

If you want to give kids a place to belong, and someone to belong to, you can't be every kid's "someone." One pastor is simply not enough.

This is why small group leaders are so important.

If you want to influence the next generation, it's not enough that you care about kids. You need to care about adults, too. You may have gone into ministry because you wanted to spend most of your time with kids. But if you really want to influence the next generation, you actually have to spend most of your time with *adults* who will spend time with kids.

IF YOUR ANSWER FOR DISCIPLESHIP IS SMALL GROUP,
AND THE PRIMARY PLACE YOU WANT A KID TO BE IS SMALL GROUP,
THEN SMALL GROUP LEADERS ARE YOUR MOST IMPORTANT
VOLUNTEERS.

Through them, you can multiply your influence to reach well beyond your own personal capacity. In fact, small group leaders are so important that maybe you shouldn't even think of them as volunteers. Maybe you should think of them as partners.

Or pastors.

When I (Elle) was seventeen, I became an SGL. At the time, growth in attendance had put our children's ministry and youth ministry in desperate need of more volunteers. So, I signed up to help. On my very first Sunday, I was given a small group of *30* fifth-grade girls.

Yep. Thirty 10-year-olds. And me.
No, that is not a recommended ratio.
And did I mention I was just a teenager?

It wasn't exactly an ideal situation. Our church would later transition to a lead small culture, but back then, we still had a long way to go. My group was so large it was difficult to manage and almost impossible to make any real connection. I hadn't received any training, so I felt nervous and unprepared. I wanted to influence kids and make a big impact, but I wasn't sure how.

Then my youth pastor said something that signaled the beginning of our church's transition. I'll never forget it.

"Small group leaders, you are the pastors of your small group."

Not . . .
volunteers,
helpers,
chaperones,
babysitters,
teachers,
discussion-leaders, or
chaos-managers.

Pastors.

If you believe THE SCOPE OF YOUR INFLUENCE IS DETERMINED BY THE SUCCESS OF YOUR LEADERS, it should motivate you to **EMPOWER THE LEADER** so they can lead.

This is something Kevin Ragsdale has been saying to North Point small group leaders for years. "When I first started ministry," Kevin told us, "I realized I could not create a great ministry experience if I tried to be the student pastor to all of our students." Knowing North Point's student ministry would quickly grow beyond the reach of his own capacity, Kevin empowered his SGLs to be the pastors of their small groups.

One pastor might not be enough to disciple every kid in your ministry, but what if instead of just *one* pastor your ministry could have 15? 30? 100? Imagine the impact you could have if you expanded your influence by empowering SGLs to partner with you in discipling kids.

But let's pause here for a second. Maybe you're not sure about this idea.

Maybe you're thinking, *But isn't pastoring and discipling my job, not theirs?*

Well . . . no.

You see, when Jesus gave us the Great Commission, the invitation to go all over the world and make disciples, He didn't give it to an exclusive group of elite Christians. He gave it to every single one of us. Not just those of us who have graduated seminary, or get a paycheck for it, or have faces on church websites. (How many of the early church leaders would have passed *that* test?)

Maybe it is scary to consider giving influence and ministry to other people. But isn't that exactly what Jesus did? For whatever reason, God put the future of His Church in the hands of human beings. In spite of our imperfection and messiness and brokenness (or maybe because of it), He decided to use us (all of us) to make disciples. God has entrusted the process of discipleship to His *whole* Church, not just the professionals.

Okay, maybe you're still a little nervous.

Maybe you're wondering, *What about the risks? What if I empower a leader and . . .*

they say things differently than I would say them?
they believe a few things differently than I believe them?
they do things I'd prefer they didn't do?

They will.

The truth is, you can't exactly control your SGLs. They will say and think and do things you probably wouldn't say or think or do. We'll spend a lot of time in the next several pages talking about how to find, select, and train your leaders so you have the right kinds of people influencing kids. Just remember: no matter how many steps you take, no matter how many parameters you set, you'll never be able to control everything that happens in small group.

Isn't it true that Jesus took the same risks with you and me? Small group leaders won't get it right every time. But let's be honest. Neither will we. God has placed His Church in the hands of imperfect people for a very long time now. And you know what? It's still here.

If you don't want to empower SGLs to disciple kids, that's okay. You don't have to. But if you don't, here's what's going to happen:

If you don't empower small group leaders, you will limit your influence to your own relational capacity. You may get to have great, focused influence on a few kids, but that's about it.

If you don't empower small group leaders, you will limit someone's perspective on God to your individual perspective on God. Your voice is important, but it's not the only voice kids need to hear.

If you don't empower small group leaders, you will limit the Church, and you will send the message to the kids and adults you influence that ministry is best left in the hands of the "professionals."

If you're okay with limiting your ministry, limiting someone's perspective on God, and limiting the Church, then don't empower small group leaders. Don't give away influence. Don't give away ministry.

But if you care about kids and want to help them have an authentic faith, then you can't do it alone. You don't have that kind of capacity. No one does. If you believe small groups are the answer, then you've got to empower leaders. If you want small groups to work, you've got to give away ministry and give away influence to your small group leaders.

Remember, this is your SGL.

We put a line under it to make one simple suggestion.
The best way to expand your influence is to empower the leader.

EXPECT MORE, NOT LESS

(Let's talk about **expectations**.)

So maybe you like this *empower the leader* idea in theory, but you're struggling with how to actually make it happen. Maybe you're thinking, *I can't see my current leaders ever taking on this kind of responsibility.* Or, *I don't know how to find the kind of leaders who are up for this kind of challenge.*

If you think it's impossible to find committed leaders, here's something to consider:

Maybe your leaders aren't committed because you haven't asked them to commit to something significant.

I (Kristen) led small groups for five years in a variety of settings: churches, para-church ministries, camps, as a volunteer, and as a staff intern. But for five years, no one ever asked me for a long-term weekly commitment. Instead, I was asked to lead for a summer, for a season, or for a school year. But the summer after my senior year of college, I interned at a ministry that raised the bar. When I offered to take a small group, they hesitated. (I had never seen a church hesitate about a volunteer before.) They wanted to make sure I understood that by taking a group for the summer, I wasn't just volunteering to see them through the summer, or the school year—but for four years. They didn't even want me to sign up for a group of freshmen if I wasn't going to make a commitment to be there on Graduation Sunday.

Seriously?

Yes. Seriously. The big commitment felt intimidating at first. But two, three, four years later, I knew I would never lead another small group any other way. I was compelled to sign up again and again, and recruit others to do the same.

If you're looking for small group leaders who are up for a big challenge, you've got to make a big ask. If you want to empower your SGLs, then you've got to expect more, not less.

Maybe your leaders aren't committed because you haven't asked them to commit to something significant.

One of the greatest indicators your ministry is moving toward a lead small culture is this: You have consistent leaders who show up in the lives of kids and students.

Sometimes we get questions about that last statement, so maybe we should clarify:
By consistent, we mean they are not rotational.
By not rotational, we mean they show up weekly.
By weekly, we mean they are there every week.

Of course, SGLs will miss some weeks. Honestly they probably should . . .
go on vacation from time to time.
stay home if they have the flu.
be present for family members even if it means skipping out on their group.

But for the most part, you are recruiting leaders who will make a weekly commitment to kids and teenagers.

"For how long?" you ask.

Well, that depends. Remember, it takes preschoolers less time to connect with a leader than it will when they are in elementary. It takes middle school students and high school students even longer to establish a pattern of trust within their group and with their leader. That's why we think the commitment should be different for SGLs in different age groups.

In most preschool and children's ministries, we encourage SGLs to stay with a group from 10 to 12 months, depending on how that ministry handles the summer.

In middle school, we encourage SGLs to stay with their group for two to three years, depending on how the ministry is structured.

In high school, we encourage SGLs to stay with their group for four to five years, in order to stay with a group of kids from freshman year through their first year of college.

If having committed weekly volunteers is a new concept for your ministry, we know transition takes time. In fact, we will cover steps to transitioning to a lead small culture at the end of the book. We know it's a big ask. But we believe the scope of your influence is determined by the success of your leaders. That is why when you empower your leaders, you will start by expecting more, not less.

> "For years I've been talking about building a family ministry team where SGLs stay with their kids over multiple years. Last year was the first time this happened. It was the largest group we've ever transitioned and I believe it was because of the familiarity."
> – **Nina Schmidgall** (All Ages)

EXPECT MORE NOT LESS, SO . . .
LEADERS KNOW THEY'RE DOING SOMETHING THAT MATTERS.

So, what do you want your leaders to do?

Hang on for just a second.

If you want committed SGLs, you can't begin with the *what* or even the *how* of leading groups. You've got to begin with *why*. *What* and *how* are important and informative. But *why* is what inspires people.

If small group leaders don't know *why* their job is significant or *why* their investment matters, they'll . . .
lose focus,
lose motivation,
stop caring,
and eventually stop showing up.

If you want leaders who are committed, they've got to know their job matters. As our friend Sue Miller has said, "No one wants to do something that's inconsequential."

Being a small group leader is anything but inconsequential. We've already said small group leaders matter. SGLs matter because kids may never know God unless they first know someone who loves God and can show them what God is like.

But small group leaders will never know just how much they matter until you let them feel responsible. And they will never feel responsible until you expect them to take responsibility.

Not just responsibility for . . .	**But responsibility to . . .**
sorting the goldfish crackers	know the details of a kid's world
assisting with a craft	connect with a kid's parents
refereeing a game	show up for significant life events
disciplining disruptive behaviors	answer tough questions
	do the work of ministry

If you want your small group leaders to know they're doing something that matters, give them a job that matters. They'll either embrace the challenge, or they'll bail.

Yes, some will bail. Not everyone is up for the challenge of being a small group leader. But that's okay. You don't need everyone to be an SGL. You just need the right people. (We'll talk more about finding and recruiting the right people a little bit later.) You need great SGLs who are ready for a big challenge because they understand how much it matters.

So, don't be afraid to ask big! There are people in your church who have been sitting in their seats just *waiting* for someone to offer them a challenge worth taking.

EXPECT MORE NOT LESS SO . . .
LEADERS KNOW WHAT YOU WANT THEM TO DO.

"When a potential small group leader shows up at your door, they're going to have two questions for you: 'What do you want me to do?' And 'How do you want me to do it?'" – **Gina McClain** (Elementary)

For the past decade, we have been talking to ministry leaders around the country about creating a culture of small groups for kids and teenagers. In these conversations, one of the number one questions leaders ask is, "What is the job of a small group leader"?

A few years ago, we set out to answer that question. For months, we met every Tuesday night to talk with small group leaders and church leaders from churches of all sizes, denominations, and demographics to clarify what a small group leader does, and what they need to know in order to succeed. The insights and conversations from those late-night meetings became Lead Small.

Simply put, we think a **small group leader** is "anyone who chooses to invest in the lives of a few to encourage authentic faith."

That's the definition.

If you want the full description, you're going to have to read *Lead Small*, but if we could just sum it up for you it would look something like this:

EVERY SGL SHOULD DO FIVE THINGS.

(1) **Be Present:**
Connect their faith to a community.

> "Someone once asked me which spiritual gifts I looked for in potential leaders. I told them I don't think there is any spiritual gift more important than the gift of showing up."
> – **Tom Shefchunas** (Middle School)

Yep. We were serious about that weekly thing. The first thing anyone must do if they want to be an SGL is show up. They need to *show up predictably*, weekly, in the lives of kids and teenagers so they can earn the kind of trust they need if they want to impact a kid's faith.

They also need to *show up mentally*. They need to be fully present with their few while they are with them. Which probably means you should send SGLs their weekly small group materials in advance. That way, they aren't trying to read while they manage their group.

And they need to *show up randomly*. SGLs need to practice being present outside the regularly scheduled, come-to-church-to-see-me times. Whether it's a card in the mail or a sign and an air horn at the Friday night football game, SGLs have a greater connection with their few when they show up for them in unexpected ways.

(2) **Create a Safe Place:**
Clarify their faith as they grow.

Small groups are messy. Anytime you put a group of kids or teenagers together in a room, with all their differences, all their personalities, and all their preferences, there's going to be some tension. But the way SGLs manage that tension has the potential to create a place that's safe enough for kids to authentically process faith.

If leaders want to create a safe place they have to *lead the group*. Every group needs a leader who isn't a peer. (That's why we don't advocate for student-led student groups.) Every group needs someone to lead, so the group will value things like acceptance, confidentiality, and honesty.

If leaders want to make their group a safe place they also have to *respect the process*. They have to understand that God is at work in every kid's life in a way that may take a little time.

Leaders who create safe places also *guard the heart*. Some things kids share in group cannot be kept confidential. We think there are three basic reasons an SGL should break confidentiality:
When a kid is hurting themselves.
When a kid is hurting someone else.
When a kid is being hurt.

Your ministry should have clear and specific guidelines for when and how an SGL breaks confidentiality. Communicate your expectations regularly. An SGL who guards the heart of a kid ensures that kid is physically and emotionally safe, both in the group and out of it.

(3) **Partner with Parents:**
Nurture an everyday faith.

This may be one of the most challenging lead small principles. Most SGLs sign up because they want to help kids or teenagers—

not their parents. But remember two things we said are true: No one has more potential to influence a kid than a parent. And every parent wants to be a better parent. So if SGLs want to make a lasting impact on the everyday faith of a kid, they have to partner with parents.

An SGL should *cue the parent* with information that will prompt a parent to do more than they might otherwise do. That probably means you, the church leader, should cue your SGLs so they can cue parents.

An SGL should also *honor the parent* in the way they talk to and about parents with their few. We tell SGLs all the time, "Never use their relational tension for your relational gain." Train your leaders to model an attitude of respect for parents in front of those they lead.

And finally, an SGL should *reinforce the family* by always valuing and not competing with the family for the kid's time, attention, and affection. If you're going to create a rhythm in your ministry that reinforces the family, make sure your SGLs have the same philosophy when it comes to significant milestones and group outings.

(**4**) **Make it Personal:**
Inspire their faith by your example.

When SGLs invest in a few, their few have a front row seat to their lives. Did that make your heart skip a beat or two? Of course it did. If you're tempted to install software to monitor the Facebook profiles and Instagram images of your SGLs, or if you're wanting to make every leader keep a record of their prayer life to submit to you monthly, it's probably because you understand the power of their example.

You can't control the spiritual habits of your leaders, but you can remind them of the importance of making it personal. If you want leaders to make it personal, you should help them *live in community*. Every SGL needs a group of peers that isn't their group of first graders.

If you want leaders to make it personal, you should help them *set priorities*. We're not just saying to help them prioritize their few, but to help them have personal and spiritual priorities that will give them the kind of personal health to lead well.

If you want leaders to make it personal, you should give them permission to *be real*. Not *too* real. Third graders probably don't need to hear about their SGLs latest breakup—in detail. They need a leader who can be authentic about . . .
their love of pimento cheese sandwiches.
their lack of knowledge about hip Indie bands.
their struggles and discoveries about faith.

One more note about setting priorities and being real: In a world filled with social media sites, your leaders are bound to share a lot of very real stuff outside the walls of your ministry that parents and kids in your ministry can see. When you set expectations for your SGLs, you may want to cover a few ground rules about their online presence. Otherwise, last week's spring break ~~ankle~~ tattoo may become a very significant part of this week's small group conversation.

Ankle

5) **Move Them Out:**
Engage their faith in a bigger story.

Small group leaders should know that what happens inside their circle will always be measured by what happens outside their circle. An SGL has significant influence in the life of a kid, but they aren't the only influence a kid needs. That's why, when it comes to their kids and teenagers, your SGLs need to *move them to someone else*.

Discipleship happens best when there's an experiential component. Especially as kids get older, they will discover more about God while they are doing what God wants them to do than they will while sitting in a circle talking about ideas. That's why SGLs need to look for ways to plug their few in to serve and *move them to be the church*.

Eventually, every group ends. Leaders take new groups, and kids grow up and move on. But when you have committed SGLs, they aren't content just to let their kids go. They want to make sure their few transition well. They want to help *move them to what's next*.

There's nothing remarkable about the five characteristics of *Lead Small*. They just simplify a few things so they're easier to talk about. The phrases act as a starting point, since everything you need to train your SGLs to do can fall into these five categories. They give you and your team a common language, so you are all on the same page. They clarify the values and expectations you have for your SGLs.

If this whole lead small thing is new to you, you might be looking at these characteristics thinking, *That's really asking* a lot *from a volunteer.* Yes. It is. That's what *expecting more, not less* is all about.

When you expect more from your SGLs, you have to be clear about what you expect them to do. Giving them a job description is great, but it's not something you can hand to an SGL one time and be done. We will talk much more about training in the next chapter, but when it comes to letting an SGL know what you want them to do, remember: You need to say it clearly. You need to say it well. And you need to say it more than once.

"The greatest challenge for our staff has been inspiring and equipping our leaders on a wide scale. That level of vision casting requires constantly weaving the vision of lead small into every available avenue of communication." – **Gina McClain** (Elementary)

"One of the best things we've done to implement a lead small culture is constant vision casting and sharing stories. People are so inspired when they hear and see the life-change happening both in kids and in those who serve." – **Amy Fenton** (Elementary)

Every fall, we have an opportunity to travel to different cities to talk with church leaders. After we wrote *Lead Small*, I (Reggie) remember speaking to a room full of leaders about these five ideas. At the end of the message, a lady came up to talk to me, and she was emotional. She had been a small group leader for 50 years. Can you imagine! This woman had given her life to investing in kids to help them develop an authentic faith. When she heard this message, she said, "I've been doing this for 50 years. I just never understood what I was doing until now."

When you help a leader know what they do, you prepare them to do it; you motivate them to do it better; you inspire them to keep doing it.

EXPECT MORE NOT LESS, SO . . .
LEADERS KNOW YOU BELIEVE THEY CAN DO IT.

Once you've given your leaders a job that matters and told them how to do it, can you guess what's next? Yep. You *let them do it*. Because until you step away and let them do it, they'll never believe *you* believe they can do it.

Let's go back to the Great Commission again. After Jesus gave us our mission, do you remember what happened? Sure you do. *He left*—at least physically. He stepped back. He let the disciples do what He asked them to do. There's something about the ascension that communicates just how much Jesus entrusts to those who follow Him. He believed the gospel would spread, disciples would be made, and the Church would move forward—by people like you and me.

In the same way, if you want empowered leaders, you need to take a giant step back and let them do what you've asked them to do.

Jesus doesn't shake His head in disbelief if we get the wrong font on the monthly posters or load the wrong lyrics into the computer. He doesn't throw up His hands in frustration and say, "Forget it, I'll take care of it" when He notices a small group has erupted into a spontaneous cheese-ball fight instead of engaging in meaningful conversation. No, Jesus entrusted His disciples with a great mission and then left them with a surprising amount of free will and authority to pull the whole thing off.

Of course, He is God. And He did send His Spirit. At the end of the day, everything is ultimately in His control. We aren't really suggesting the mission and ministry of the church is completely run by people. Neither are we suggesting that you let your Kindergarten SGLs run their group like a private club. They are still responsible to you and your ministry team.

We are just suggesting there will be moments when . . .
you become less of a big deal, so small group leaders can be a bigger deal.
you take less responsibility so they can do something that matters.
you don't solve the problem because you know they are capable on their own.

If your small group leaders are going to believe they can do it, they've got to know *you* believe they can do it. And they'll never know *you* believe they can do it until you actually *let* them do it.

When you get in the habit of expecting more from your small group leaders, your small group leaders will lead in ways you never expected.

PLAY
FAVORITES

(Let's talk about **training**.)

Teachers probably shouldn't play favorites with their students.
Parents probably shouldn't play favorites with their kids.
But if you want to empower the leader, you've got to play favorites with your small group leaders.

Whether you realize it or not, you *already* play favorites in other areas of your life.

Don't believe it? Okay, think about this: How many Facebook friends do you have? The average adult has around 338. (Yes, we looked it up.) So, let's say you are average. (Of course you're not average. You're probably way more popular than average—but just play along). How many of those 338 friends have ever been to your home? How many did you share a meal with this month? How many did you text this week?

Now, before you get worked up because you think you're a terrible friend and need to immediately plan a 338-person dinner party for next weekend, hang on. That's not the point.

It's okay that you haven't invested recently in all 338 of your Facebook friends. This doesn't make you a terrible friend because, as you might recall, your capacity is limited. You can't possibly be expected to have quality relationships with 338 people. So, you play favorites. You have an inner circle of people who *do* come to your home, who you *do* share meals with, and whose names populate the "most recent" screens on your cell phone. You invest the most in the relationships that mean the most to you.

Sometimes, playing favorites is a good thing.

Remember all the volunteers we said you have? There are some who . . .

welcome kids at the door.
help families register and sign in.
keep your area safe.
run your production.
feed everyone.
lead small groups.

Regardless of the size of your ministry, you probably have some volunteers who help you make your weekly environments happen. We know you appreciate every single one of those volunteers. But while all volunteers are important, your small group leaders should be your favorites. They are your inner circle.

Remember, your relational capacity is around eight to 10 people. And just like you don't have the capacity to invest in every kid, you might not have the capacity to equally invest in every volunteer. If you have more than eight volunteers on your team. . . . (You know where we're going with this, don't you?)

Once you've surpassed your relational capacity with your volunteers, you can no longer . . .
know every name.
remember every birthday.
follow every story.
keep up with every need.
pastor every volunteer.

You need to prioritize your influence to focus on the volunteers who matter most. You need to prioritize your SGLs because there is simply more at stake with your SGLs. Their responsibility is the greatest because you've given them the most influence in kids' lives. And because you're expecting the most from them, you've got to give them more than you give any other volunteer.

More time.
More training.
More care.

Think of it this way: If you want your small group leaders to give kids a place to belong, then maybe you should go first by giving SGLs a place to belong. Just like your kids and students need "someone," your SGLs need "someone," too.

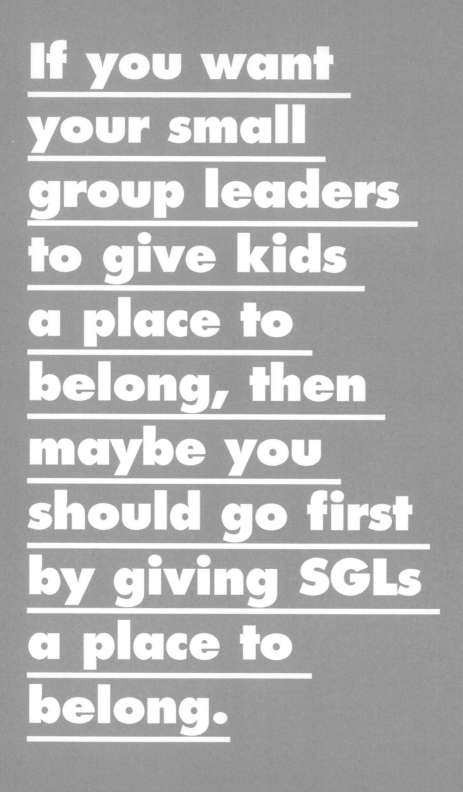

If you want your small group leaders to give kids a place to belong, then maybe you should go first by giving SGLs a place to belong.

That's why you need someone who feels directly responsible for your SGLs. Let's call that person a coach.

Maybe that coach is you. Maybe it's not.
Maybe it's someone already on your team, or maybe it's someone you still need to find.
Maybe it's a staff person, or maybe it's a volunteer.
Maybe it's one person, or maybe it's several.

Regardless of the size and organization of your ministry, small group leaders need *someone* who prioritizes them. They need someone who gives them time, training, and care. They need someone who knows what's going on in their groups and in their lives, too. They need a coach.

So, what is a coach?
A coach is someone who is responsible for managing and shepherding SGLs.

A coach manages. Small group leaders need a coach because they need someone to manage the details that go into creating a great small group experience.

SGLs need someone who . . .
knows when they show up.
monitors the size of their group.
thinks about the dynamics of their group.
provides the supplies they need to make group happen.

But managing can't be *all* a coach does. That model just won't work. It's not enough.

A coach shepherds. Small group leaders don't just need someone to care about the management of their group. They need someone to care about *them*.

SGLs need someone who . . .
listens to their stories.
knows the name of their dog.
cares about their job changes, new babies, and big moves.
takes care of them before they show up to take care of kids.

The best model for a coach is a mixture of manager and shepherd. In our experience, the best coaches are 50 percent administrative and 50 percent relational. They manage details, and they care for people.

So, how many coaches do you need?

We're back to that relational capacity again. You can do the math. If you have six SGLs, maybe you incorporate coaching responsibilities as part of your or another staff member's job description. Or maybe you have someone you have recruited to serve in this capacity. If you have 15 small group leaders, you need to develop a coaching system. Recruit three coaches, and put someone in charge of those coaches.

It's a relational numbers game. We think the winning formula looks something like this.

8 LEADERS = 1 COACH

But remember how you organize to be organic? This formula isn't mentioned anywhere in Acts, so if you have nine leaders to one coach it doesn't mean you aren't biblical. Just discover what works best for your ministry.

So, what's your solution?
How can you arrange or rearrange your team to give your SGLs a coach? Do you need to make a new hire? Do you need to recruit a new team of volunteers?

Unfortunately, we can't answer those questions for you. But we can tell you this: A great coaching strategy will meet three significant needs for your small group leaders.

They need to be known, trained, and celebrated.

....

WHEN YOU PLAY FAVORITES . . .
YOUR SMALL GROUP LEADERS MAKE IT ONTO YOUR SHORT LIST.

SGLs need to be known.
I (Kristen) began leading my second small group in the fall of 1999. Only a few weeks after moving 832 miles away from home to begin my freshman year of college, I found a local ministry and signed up to lead a small group. I was excited to do something that would matter and wanted to invest in the lives of a few. We met every Tuesday for a large group program and every Thursday after school for small group. We

did book studies. We had small group parties. I went to their basketball games and got to know their parents. On the surface, anyone looking in would have said things were working well. But the problem was, I was on course for a major crash, and no one leading that ministry knew. As a student athlete with a job and a small group, I had filled every hour of every day with one commitment after another. I hadn't yet found my own community or made time for friends. I felt more alone than ever. During one of our weekly large group environments, I remember looking around the room and thinking, *No one here knows me.* I knew them. I knew my few. But I wasn't truly known by anyone who I served with or served under.

Since one of the five roles of a small group leader is to "make it personal," someone on your ministry team should have the responsibility of knowing your SGLs personally. Your coaches don't have to be a marriage counselor, chemistry tutor, personal shopper, or party planner for your SGLs. Coaches don't have to spend long hours listening to the story of a best friend's, brother's, ex-fiance's latest vacation. But they should know the leader in a way that is more than purely functional.

Let's put it this way: Someone should know your SGL
less than their therapist
but more than their car mechanic.

WHEN YOU PLAY FAVORITES . . .
YOUR SMALL GROUP LEADERS MAKE IT ONTO YOUR WEEKLY TO-DO LIST.

SGLs need to be trained.
Think for a minute about all the things you need to do every week to make your environments happen and keep your ministry moving.

Okay. Now, stop.

That's a long list! What if we said there are a few more things you should add to your weekly to-do list? Things like . . .
giving SGLs their small group materials in advance.
casting and recasting vision to SGLs.
cueing SGLs to connect with their few.
training SGLs so they can be better at what they do.

Coaching SGLs takes time. SGLs don't just need to be known; they need to know what they need to know.

Now, if you're getting nervous because you're visualizing a complicated series of training videos, safety classes, and volunteer meetings . . . relax. We think that sounds horrible, too. Thanks to technology, there are plenty of ways to train and re-inspire your SGLs year-round without filling their calendars with meetings and making them hate you. Email, texting, social media, blogs, and video-sharing sites have revolutionized the way we communicate with each other. That means our opportunities to train leaders in new and creative ways are practically limitless. You can decide how best to train your SGLs; we just know you should train them.

Train your SGLs annually.
Each year, you have one good opportunity to bring SGLs together for an official "kick-off." But have you ever noticed how difficult it is to plan an event that pleases *everyone?* Some come because they want to be inspired. Some come looking for a date. Others come for the food. How do you plan a training event that connects with as many people as possible? Here's a simple formula we've found to be effective:

1/3 CONNECTION + 1/3 INFORMATION +1/3 INSPIRATION
. . . and always have food.

CONNECTION
No small group leader should lead alone. They need to know you and your staff. They need to know each other. They need to know that leading a small group is sometimes a team effort. So, if you plan an annual event to kick off the year, plan a little time for them to connect.

INFORMATION
There are probably some logistical things you will want your leaders to know about you, about your ministry, and about your church. They need to know where to go, what to wear, and how to sign in. If they work in the toddler room, they may need to know which bathroom to use. Don't spend time going over everything you want them to know. No one likes showing up for a meeting just to hear what you could have sent in an email. But take the time you need to answer their questions and give them the information they need to be successful.

INSPIRATION

You've made a big ask of your SGLs. If you want them to know they have a significant role in your ministry, now is one—of many—times to tell them. Inspire your leaders to be present, create a safe place, partner with parents, make it personal, and move them out. Tell stories. Show videos. Make a really big deal about what they are about to do for the kids in their group.

Here's something you might want to consider: Toddlers aren't the same as teenagers. Wait, you already knew that. So, when you inspire SGLs, consider making it specific for the age group they will work with this year. We believe SGLs who work with preschoolers can do something remarkable for kids at that age that is unique to that phase of life. The same is true for elementary, middle school, and high school. SGLs at each age group have a unique role to play. Sometimes we say it this way:

Preschool	Elementary	Middle school	High school
EMBRACE	**ENGAGE**	**SHIFT**	**MOBILIZE**
them to see God's love and meet God's family.	them to trust God's character and live out God's story.	them to own their faith and never do faith alone.	them to deeper discipleship and greater mission.

You can put your own spin on it. Just remember to let your leaders know *why* what they do is a significant part of your ministry. Use your annual kick off event to inspire them with language you will continue to use throughout the year. This is the set-up. Everything that comes after will be how you reinforce what matters again and again.

Train your SGLs seasonally.

No matter how well you inspire leaders at your kick off event, there's a good chance the inspiration will fade over time—like maybe by next week. Just like you have a scope and cycle for the kids in your ministry, you probably need a cycle to help you train and inspire your leaders on a regular basis. Think about the natural rhythm and flow of the year. As you train your leaders, you should have a monthly focus that corresponds to those natural rhythms. We came up with one example of what a seasonal training plan for SGLs might look like:

AUGUST	SEPTEMBER	OCTOBER
5 Principles of Lead Small	Create a Safe Place	Move them Out (to serve)

NOVEMBER	DECEMBER	JANUARY
Special Event	Partner with Parents	Make it Personal

FEBRUARY	MARCH	APRIL
Create a Safe Place	Be Present	Partner with Parents

MAY	JUNE	JULY
Move them Out (to what's next)	Make it Personal	Be Present

Maybe it's because I (Elle) have so many college-aged SGLs, but I've found it helps our SGLs when we think about training in three semesters. We often begin a semester with a small group leader training event where, among other things, we give each SGL a list of goals we hope they accomplish during that semester. We try to keep the list simple and focused, using the goals as a way to call back the vision and job description of an SGL. We might set five goals for the semester, like: Have a party with your small group; write every kid in your group a postcard and the church will mail them for you; or come to a small group leader and parent breakfast. If an SGL completes all of their goals for the semester, they get a gift card to one of their favorite places. It's been an easy way for us to switch up our approach to training. And who doesn't like incentives?

Train your SGLs weekly.
You can and should do something every week to train your SGLs. Whoever is responsible for your leaders should have a weekly to-do list that looks something like this:
MONDAY: Write and mail an SGL a note.
TUESDAY: Take an SGL out for coffee.
WEDNESDAY: Post about your monthly series to Instagram.
THURSDAY: Send all SGLs a weekly email.
SATURDAY: Text SGLs important information.
SUNDAY: Brag about groups publicly on Facebook, Instagram, and Twitter.

Every time you send small group curriculum or discussion guides, write an email, post to social media, text, or connect with your SGLs in any way, you have an opportunity to train them in bite-sized pieces. There are countless simple things you can do every week to give your leaders the tools and knowledge they need to help them be better small group leaders.

WHEN YOU PLAY FAVORITES . . .
YOUR SMALL GROUP LEADERS MAKE IT ONTO YOUR PARTY LIST.

SGLs need to be celebrated.
We have one more list to talk about. For this last list, take a moment to think about all the things your ministry has celebrated recently. What's on that list? What are the things you have acknowledged publicly and privately? What kinds of things have you thrown parties over?

Maybe you celebrated the number of kids baptized last month, or the amount of canned goods collected for the community food drive, or that only one kid got hit in the face at the dodgeball tournament. You've probably celebrated some great things recently. But how often do you celebrate your SGLs?

What you celebrate reveals what you value. Think about what your recent celebrations reveal about your priorities. If small group leaders didn't show up on your party list, what did? Attendance? Events? Large group environments? There is nothing wrong with any of these things. But if SGLs are your favorites, you should celebrate them like favorites.

A great coach prioritizes the celebration of small group leaders because small group leaders are worth throwing parties for.

CELEBRATE THEM PUBLICLY
When you play favorites with your small group leaders, you bring their stories and their wins into the public eye. You celebrate them from every platform in your church: in staff meetings, in front of parents, to other SGLs, in front of kids, and online. If you want to empower SGLs, you need to reward what you want to see repeated. So, celebrate the leaders who are doing it well by spotlighting their stories. Let the vision spread by their example.

CELEBRATE THEM PRIVATELY
You can't only celebrate your small group leaders publicly. When you see an SGL do something great, acknowledge it with a handwritten note, a quick email, or a compliment in the hallway. Let them know you noticed.

CELEBRATE THEM RANDOMLY
Whether it's birthdays, anniversaries, holidays, end-of-the-year appreciations, or just because, create opportunities to celebrate small group leaders unexpectedly and randomly. Remember, being an SGL is a big job. That unexpected celebration might be just what they need in the moment they need it.

When you get in the habit of coaching SGLs by playing favorites, you are doing for them what you are asking them to do for their few.

WIN BEFORE
YOU BEGIN

(Let's talk about **recruitment**.)

Imagine for a moment you're back in high school gym class . . . during the dodgeball unit. You pull on the T-shirt and mesh shorts you probably haven't washed since August, tie your shoelaces tight, and jog toward the basketball courts where your physical education teacher is waiting. He says he's going to "randomly" appoint two team captains, but since his selections are this year's starting quarterback for the football team and a far less celebrated Rubik's Cube aficionado wearing a fedora, you suspect your gym teacher may be mistaken about the definition of *random*.

Team selections begin.
QB drafts one of his teammates—an offensive lineman.
Fedora drafts his buddy from the debate team.
QB picks his girlfriend—starting pitcher for the girl's softball team.
Fedora selects the kid who custom-coded the school website.

We could keep going, but that's probably all the information you need. If you were placing bets (which we know you never do), you'd probably know which team to pick. One of these teams wins before the game starts.

If you want to win a high school dodgeball game, you've got to stack your team with the right strengths. But if you want to win at small groups, you need to stack your team with small group leaders who have the right potential.

So, what makes a great small group leader?
It's simple.

They've got to follow Jesus.
They've got to like kids.
They've got to pass their background check.

Okay. That's an oversimplification. But really . . .

They don't need to be a 20-year veteran of the Christian faith.
They don't have to be Bible experts, or pass a theological aptitude test.
They don't have to display a particular set of special spiritual gifts.
They don't even need to be cool.

When I (Kristen) was in high school, there was one leader who stood out from the rest. His name was Ralph, and when I think of him, I remember a thinly haired, scrawny man with a mustache and jean shorts. He stood out not only because he was absolutely the least trendy man in the room, but also because he literally stood outside our youth group. (It was called Power Source if you want to know.) He stood by the door as we came in, and he welcomed us. When he saw someone new, he talked to them. When a kid wanted to sit outside and smoke, he sat with them. (I'm sure some people questioned Ralph's judgment in the teenagers he allowed himself to hang around.) But Ralph formed the most unlikely connections. Students who might not have ever come back to church a second or third time came back because he was there and because they knew he cared about them.

So, you know that nerdy science teacher? He might become an instant hero when he brings his pet axolotls to group to illustrate the wonder of creation. Or what about that elderly woman you never thought could have any relevance to high school girls? Watching her serve might remind you that having influence in a kid's life is actually less about being cool than it is about being present.

The point is this: Don't be too quick to disqualify someone from leading.
ANYONE CAN BE A GREAT SGL.
BUT NOT EVERYONE *SHOULD* BE AN SGL.

This idea isn't revolutionary. Your church probably already does this in other areas of ministry.

Think about it:
If you can't carry a tune, you should probably not join the choir.
If you don't know how to set up a Twitter account, you shouldn't be in charge of the church's social media presence.
If you're awkwardly shy, you should definitely not be on the greeter team.
And if you cry over weird smells, you probably shouldn't work with babies—or middle school boys.

We aren't saying some people shouldn't serve; everyone can serve somewhere. It's just that not everyone is meant to be an SGL. Your small group leaders are critical volunteers, and you can't afford to have leaders who aren't equipped or committed to the job. There's too much at stake.

If you're going to win before you begin, you've got to control the quality of the leaders on your team.

So now that you know what it takes to be a great small group leader, you may be wondering, "*Where are these people? I need them! NOW.*"

You're not alone. If there's one characteristic every church has in common, it's probably this: No one has enough small group leaders. No matter how many you have, you'll always need more. You will never be done recruiting SGLs.

And since recruiting SGLs will be an ongoing part of your job until you become famous or move to the beaches of Caicos, we want to give you a few recruiting principles. Unlike dodgeball, the success of your ministry isn't connected to physical strength and agility. It is connected to how well you recruit, screen, and prepare your SGLs before they begin to lead. If you want to get in the habit of winning before you begin, there are a few things you should do.

....

YOU WIN BEFORE YOU BEGIN WHEN . . .
YOUR BEST LEADERS RECRUIT YOUR BEST LEADERS.

One year when I (Reggie) was leading our family ministry team at North Point, our preschool environment was in need of SGLs. Okay—that happened every year. But this particular year, early in our ministry, our pastor, Andy Stanley, asked for leaders from the platform. If you've ever heard Andy ask for volunteers, you know he can be pretty compelling. In a single day, after just one message, we had over 300 leaders signed up to serve preschoolers. It's good news for you that we aren't advocating this as your model because I'm not sure anyone else can get that kind of result after one message.

We were happy with the results. We had more than enough leaders, so I assumed our recruitment troubles were over. At the end of the year, however, when it came time to reassign groups, only three of those 300 leaders remained. When I asked the Groups Directors what was different about the leaders who stayed, they told me, "Those leaders are a different kind of leader. They recruited their friends to serve with them, and they feel more ownership in their role." So, I responded by asking our preschool team to go find 20 more leaders like those leaders. Instead of recruiting 300, it may be important to start by recruiting the right 20. If you recruit the right few, they will help you recruit and keep the rest.

When I helped write *The 7 Practices of Effective Ministry*, we shared how, when we started North Point, we had few relationships or connections to potential volunteers. So, we began asking our existing SGLs to help us recruit new SGLs. At meetings, we handed out index cards and asked our SGLs to write down the names of two or three friends who could do what our SGLs were doing. Then we challenged them to recruit at least one of those friends to join them. We were amazed at the number of new volunteers our existing volunteers recruited when we leveraged their personal network.

When you want to find and attract the best leaders, casting a wide net isn't always helpful. An announcement from the platform or in a bulletin might draw a crowd, but in the long run, the time you will spend sorting through a huge number of applicants can be more work than it's worth. When you inspire volunteers to join you in the recruitment process, however, you can cast your net to a more targeted group of people. You demonstrate trust in your SGLs when you ask for their input, and you make recruiting a team effort. And because your SGLs know what they're doing matters and know what it takes to be a great leader, they can help you recruit leaders who will have longevity. Because, chances are, your best leaders will respond to a personal invitation, not an announcement.

❝

"Small group leaders who love what they do will attract other small group leaders who have the same heart and passion for engaging students and building relationships." – **Jeffrey Wallace** (High School)

"We recruit most of our SGLs by one-on-one recruiting—mainly by leaders recruiting other leaders. When our leaders see the value of their position, their passion overflows." – **Adam Duckworth** (Elementary)

"We ask leaders to find their own replacement. When a group gets too large, the leaders invite someone to step in and co-lead for a season. Eventually, as that group continues to grow, the new leader takes half of the group as their own." – **Bobbi Miller** (Elementary)

❞

It will take work and time, but you can cultivate leaders who recruit other leaders. How? Find your best SGLs and have this conversation: "We need more people like you. Who do you know?"

YOU WIN BEFORE YOU BEGIN WHEN . . .
RECRUITING LEADERS IS A PROCESS, NOT AN EVENT.

Wouldn't it be great if recruiting small group leaders was as simple as an event? Imagine how fantastic it would be if we could write "Recruitment Day!" on our calendars, knowing this one day would yield all the SGLs we'd need for the entire year. What if we could simply list the number of SGLs we needed and stand back while a mob of enthusiastic, perfectly qualified people rushed to sign up? What if we could rest our heads on our pillows at night knowing we wouldn't even have to *think* about recruiting for another 365 days because, of course, our perfect new SGLs would never quit, move away, or do anything that would force us to fire them?

If you aren't sighing with longing—even a little bit—right now, you probably didn't read that last paragraph very closely.

Recruiting SGLs isn't an event we can compartmentalize to a single day each year. It's a multi-step process.

As we talk to ministry leaders around the country about their system for recruiting, training, and integrating SGLs, we've discovered that most churches follow the same basic six-step process. It may seem like a lot of steps just to place a volunteer, but this isn't any volunteer. You should be selective about who you ask to be an SGL; you're giving them a really big job!

1. Invitation
The first step in recruiting is, of course, to *ask*. Whether you're asking from a platform or in a one-on-one conversation, remember: You're looking for leaders who want to do something that matters so ask big, because great leaders respond to big challenges.

2. Orientation
Before a potential volunteer can commit to being a small group leader, they need to know what's expected of them. Some churches host

group orientation events. Others keep their orientations to one-on-one conversations. However you structure your orientation, there are four things you'll want to do:

- Revisit the vision.
- Familiarize them with your environment.
- Communicate the expectations and commitment.
- Let them make the next move.

3. Application and Background Checks

If a potential leader is still interested after they've attended an orientation and heard the expectations, their next step is to complete an application and give you permission to run a background check. If your orientation scared them away, that's okay. They weren't the right fit. But if they've taken that next step, process their background check and review their application and references carefully. Do you see any red flags? If so, you'll need to have a conversation with them. If not, schedule an interview.

4. Interview

An interview is your last opportunity to filter a potential SGL before they actually encounter a kid, so it's serious. Here are three things to consider during an interview:

- **Hear from them.** Ask them to share their story. Why do they want to be an SGL? Listen to their answers to see if they've caught the vision, understand the expectations, and are ready to make the commitment.
- **Let them hear from you.** An interview with a potential SGL isn't an executive corporate hire. Relax. Have a conversation. Make a new friend! If this person is going to join your team, it helps if you like each other. Don't be afraid to share your own story and let them ask questions of their own.
- **Consider their placement.** Up until this point, you may not have discussed where this person will serve. Which age group? Is there a potential co-leader? Now that you have a read on their story and their personality, begin to identify which kids and leaders might be a good fit.

5. Training

Before you turn anyone loose with a group of kids, they need a little training. This isn't the only time you will train them. This is just the training they need to get started. Give your potential SGL (preferably, in writing) the vision, expectations, code of conduct, and details of their role—one more time. We recommend having them sign a commitment stating they've read and understood the policies and expectations you've laid out for them. Establishing clear goals up front will make conversations easier if you need to confront unmet expectations or breaches in conduct.

6. Apprenticeship
When a potential leader makes it this far, it's time for them to get their feet wet and actually begin interacting with kids. This is such a significant part of the process, we'll talk more about this in just a second.

> "We never randomly place leaders in groups because we want it to be their choice. If it's their choice, we think they'll be much more likely to own it and stick with it." – **Jeffrey Wallace** (High School)

Recruiting isn't just a multi-step process. It's a year-round process, too. Leaders quit, move away, or transition to other ministries. Attendance spikes and groups grow. When these things happen, you'll need more leaders. There are also leaders who move into town, or decide they are ready to take a small group—even though it's the middle of the year. Never turn a potential SGL away just because it's January. You may not have the perfect placement ready for them, but when you think about recruitment as a year-round process, you get into the habit of recruiting leaders annually, seasonally, monthly, and weekly. Finding and placing SGLs will be an ongoing, never-ending part of what you do.

> "We recruit through vision casting in our adult service, emails, blog posts. . . any and every way possible to keep the mission and vision out there." – **Amy Fenton** (Elementary)
>
> "We create several short-term service opportunities every year, where we recruit leaders to serve for just a day (like on Christmas or Easter), or for a few months in the summer. If we see someone who impresses us, we invite them to continue serving with us after their short-term commitment runs out." – **Bobbi Miller** (Elementary)

YOU WIN BEFORE YOU BEGIN WHEN . . .
LEADERS PRACTICE LEADING BEFORE THEY LEAD.

As we said, the final step in the process of recruiting new leaders is apprenticeship. This is important because you can't know if a leader is ready to lead their own group until you (or someone you trust) actually see them do it. So, before you launch a leader into full-time SGL status, set them up with a veteran leader and let them practice.

A new leader needs the opportunity to practice while they're learning how to lead a group, but they also need feedback from both the veteran leader who observes them and the coach who oversees them. Make it clear both to the new leader and the veteran leader what this time of apprenticeship is meant to do: reproduce leaders who are doing it well. The veteran leaders need to lead by their example, while the new leader needs to learn.

"Prospective SGLs are more successful when they make a solid connection with someone who can coach, encourage, and challenge them. Otherwise, the prospective leader might develop their own approach to leading a group that may not be consistent with your vision."
– **Gina McClain** (Elementary)

How does a veteran leader apprentice a new SGL?

They lead and let the new SGL watch.
They lead alongside the new SGL.
The new SGL leads while they watch.

Apprenticeship takes time, but if you want the very best leaders, it's worth the investment.

YOU WIN BEFORE YOU BEGIN WHEN . . .
YOU CREATE A PLACE WHERE LEADERS WANT TO BE.

Sure, you work for your ministry. But if you are recruiting great SGLs year-round, you may need to make your ministry work for you. Maybe your best recruitment tool isn't a single fancy piece of paper or a compelling video or a church-wide campaign. It's your volunteer culture that attracts and keeps SGLs. Consider this . . .

Do your leaders love coming to your environments? Are they having fun?
Do your SGLs like each other? Are they finding community with other leaders?
Do they feel prepared, trained, and supported?
Do they feel heard and valued?

If you want excellent leaders, you'll need to create an excellent culture of leaders. That means you put a priority on how you value your leaders' time. You celebrate them. You give them insider information. You give them doughnuts, T-shirts, wristbands, fake mustaches, and whatever it takes to make them feel like they are your favorite people on the planet.

Creating an excellent culture also means making hard decisions. Despite your best efforts to find and recruit great leaders, you may still find yourself with someone who doesn't need to be an SGL in your ministry. Sometimes you have to protect the integrity of your culture by transitioning an SGL to a different role. If you don't let go of the wrong leaders, you might not attract the right leaders.

You may have many reasons for asking an SGL to transition to another volunteer position. Here are four:

An SGL can't meet the expectations of their role.
An SGL can't connect with an age group.
An SGL can't align with the direction of the ministry.
An SGL can't live the way you want them to lead kids to live.

In any of those situations, it may be time for an SGL to transition to a different volunteer position. Transitioning an SGL will never be easy. But the more clearly and frequently you communicate your expectations to leaders up front, the easier these conversations will be when they happen.

Remember, your SGLs are some of your most significant volunteers. They are the "someone" you're intentionally placing in the life of a kid or teenager to shape their faith.

When you make it a habit to win before you begin, you recruit better leaders who will recruit better leaders.

BEHAVIOR

CREATE THE EXPERIENCE

BELIEF:

The truth of your message is amplified
by the depth of your relationships

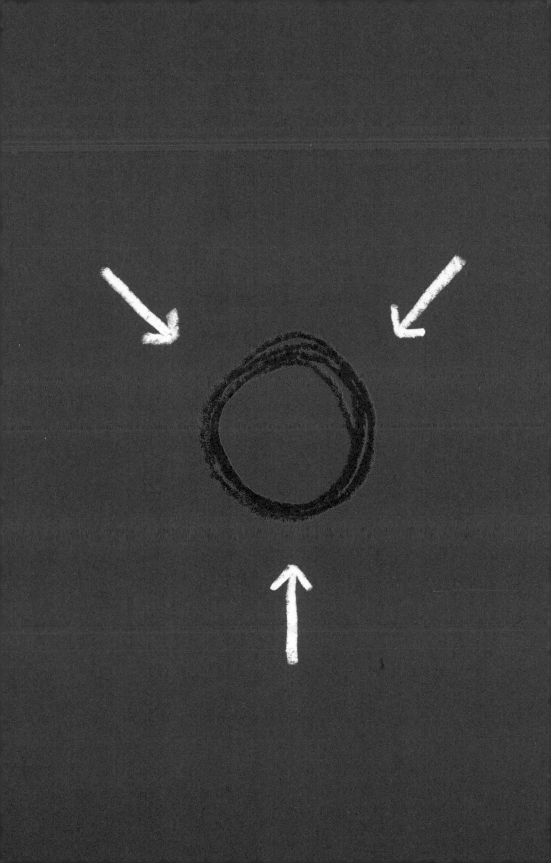

CREATE THE EXPERIENCE

Picture this. You run into the grocery store for some Double Stuf Oreos because you're out, and you really can't go another day without Double Stuf Oreos. You get to the checkout line. You're checking Twitter on your phone and scanning the tabloids to see if there are any great stories you can incorporate into this week's message. Then, as you scan your credit card, the cashier casually asks you, "On a scale of one to ten, how do you feel like your prayer life is going?"

No?

Okay, try this one. You're at the gym working out—maybe for the first time in a few months. The guy next to you is doing an intense routine so you step aside to give him a little more room. He looks over at you, takes his earbuds out, smiles and says, "*The prudent see danger and take refuge, but the foolish keep going and suffer for it.*"

A little creepy?

If you don't think so, this next point may escape you. But for the rest of you, those who would be tempted to order a workout video that can be safely done inside your own home far away from smiley gym man, consider this: There are some things we earn the right to say in someone's life.

Maybe that's why when it comes to discipling the next generation, it's probably not a good idea to share your ideas about the Apocalypse before you know a kid's last name. Or why you might want to save your insights on moral purity until after you know the names of their parents. Or why you might not want to explain the benevolence of a loving Father before you know what happened in their world last week.

It's not that those truths aren't important.
It's not even that those truths can't be shared by a communicator on a platform.
It's just that some truths are better processed in the context of a relationship.

You will always be able to communicate truth more effectively when you are communicating that truth through someone who has an ongoing, weekly relationship with a kid or teenager.

As church leaders, we feel tremendous responsibility to communicate the greatest message on the planet. We are driven by the mission to help every kid and every teenager understand they are loved by their Creator. We want them to understand that He sent His Son to die for them to give them a full life, both now and for eternity. We also believe by helping kids understand God's story of redemption and biblical principles of wisdom, we can help them have a better future.

So, we care about the message. A lot. But if we care about the message in a way that makes us lose sight of who we are trying to impact, we may start to behave a little like that creeper at the gym.

But you're not a creeper at the gym. You believe the **truth** of your message has greater potential when it's communicated in the context of consistent relationships.

Because you believe THE TRUTH OF YOUR MESSAGE CAN BE AMPLIFIED BY THE DEPTH OF YOUR RELATIONSHIPS, you should **CREATE THE EXPERIENCE** every week to enhance small group connection.

Building a ministry where small group is the answer for discipleship means more than just organizing your ministry to connect kids in consistent groups with consistent leaders. It means more than recruiting and training SGLs who understand their role. It also means you will be intentional about the way you create a weekly experience.

Before you get too excited about rethinking your weekly experience, let's be clear. We aren't going to suggest you disciple preschoolers with a weekly adventure to Chuck E Cheese or that you help a kid trust in Jesus by taking them out to the park to play kickball or that the best plan to encourage a teenager to own their own faith is by organized laser tag.

Those things are all great. And you'll want to plan for some of that in the context of your calendar year if you want to help foster strategic relationships. But more than that, you *should* plan a weekly experience where kids can worship, hear biblical truth presented in a relevant and direct way, and process that experience in small group. A lead small culture doesn't mean you get rid of weekly programming. It simply means you change the way you prepare and evaluate your weekly experience when you understand the goal is always what happens in small group.

We've already said . . .
the primary place you want a kid to be is small group.
your answer for discipleship is small group.
your most important volunteer is the small group leader.

As you plan your weekly experience, that means you will begin with the small group in mind. The problem is, when all is said and done, you can't control what happens in a small group. You can't force relationships to work. You can't make relational ministry predictable or perfect.

When your success is predicated on a relational connection, it can be tricky to plan and even harder to evaluate. But that doesn't mean it's impossible. Sure, there's a level of it that's out of your control. If you're a fan of a good calendar and a spreadsheet, if you like a weekly to-do list and you rest better at night knowing it was a productive day, don't worry. There are still some things you can control, and it's actually a lot more productive to focus on those.

YOU CAN'T make a kid talk during group,	→	**BUT YOU CAN** create a message that is likely to provoke a conversation.
YOU CAN'T make kids have fun with each other,	→	**BUT YOU CAN** create a physical space that appeals to your audience.
YOU CAN'T make leaders relate to their few,	→	**BUT YOU CAN** evaluate the group connection to see where you can improve.

You can't create perfect small groups, but you can create the experience every week. And as you create and refine, you should consider three things that make small group experiences win:
content,
context and
connection.

HAVE IMAGINARY CONVERSATIONS

(Let's talk about your **content**.)

I (Kristen) remember very clearly the day I discovered the value of imaginary conversations. I wasn't playing Strawberry Shortcake as a child, or sitting in a psych ward. I was leading a small group of eleventh-grade girls.

You might think there are some similarities between an eleventh-grade small group and the psych ward, but that's a different conversation. That night in small group, I asked a question that was followed by silence. No problem. As a fairly veteran leader, I was comfortable with the silence. I let it sit . . . and sit . . . and sit. And then I began to realize this wasn't the kind of silence where they were processing their answers. Instead, they were exchanging confused looks and uncomfortably averting their eyes. Then one savvy sarcastic girl spoke up. "So, Kristen, can *you* answer that question?" Immediately all eyes were on me. Now it was my turn to be uncomfortably silent. No. I could not answer the question. It was a weird question. I just hadn't noticed until I put myself into my girls' place—or rather, they put me in it—and I had to respond.

After that day, I never asked a small group question again without reading through the list first. (Okay, that's not true. Some weeks are just busy.) But now I make every effort to have an imaginary small group conversation before I have an actual one. It changes what I will say in the room.

If you've ever . . .
sat through an interview,
broken up with a boyfriend,
called home with bad news,
proposed to a girlfriend,
or confronted a friend,
you have probably had an imaginary conversation.

You know that what you say in the moment can be said better if you anticipate what you are going to say (or not say).

You wanted a little bit of rehearsal time. You know that what you say in the moment can be said better if you anticipate what you are going to say (or not say).

As a church leader, you will also need to have some imaginary conversations if you want to create a message that can be experienced in small group.

Remember, you have the greatest message of all time. But if you're lucky, you will get forty hours this next year to tell a kid everything they need to know about God. That's not a lot. When you factor in sports, holidays, and shared custody, you will probably have far less time with your average attender to communicate everything you need to communicate.

That's a lot of pressure.

So, I'm going to say something that might sound a little harsh, but here it is: You're irresponsible if you aren't strategically planning your message. Yes, you will have opportunities to influence kids and teenagers outside of your programming. But your weekly programming is the environment where you have their attention (at varying levels) for somewhere around an hour. So, you should do everything you can do to make the most of that hour.

You need a comprehensive plan.
You need a clear bottom line.
You need relevant examples.
You need visual illustrations.
You need funny jokes.
You need practical applications.

Now, if you're starting to shut down and have some imaginary conversations with us about how some of the expectations in this book are just a little unrealistic, let us step in and respond. We aren't trying to paint an impossible picture. If you are working to improve your structure so you can support relational connection, and you are recruiting, training, and leading exceptional leaders who can be present in the lives of a few on a weekly basis, then you are a very busy person. We get that. That's why we think you shouldn't create your own curriculum. You should use a pre-designed curriculum and customize it.

Okay, fair disclaimer: those of us who are writing this book also create curriculum. So, maybe you think it's self-serving for us to say you ought to use one.

But let's put this in perspective for a minute:

 YOU HAVE AROUND 40 WORK HOURS THIS WEEK, WHICH MEANS YOU WILL PROBABLY SPEND . . .

15 hours in meetings with staff and SGLs,

10 hours answering email,

½ hour testing the fog machine so it doesn't set off the fire alarm,

1 hour disabling the fire alarm,

5 hours in conversations with parents and kids,

½ hour meeting about the next meeting,

10 hours setting up for, working, and cleaning up after programming,

1 hour making one more run to Costco for Goldfish Crackers and Dixie cups.

That leaves about **-3 hours** to think about your message this week.

On our team, we have twelve full-time staff who work directly to plan, write, script, act, edit, and produce monthly curriculum . . . for one age-group. That's over **two thousand man-hours** invested every month for creating a strategic, relevant, engaging message.

We do what we can do with our experiences and creative abilities so you can do what only you can do: connect on the frontlines with leaders and kids.

Whether you use our curriculum or someone else's, it just makes sense to let someone give you a starting place. If you're in a unique situation where your role requires you to write your own curriculum, maybe you should appeal to leadership for some creative ways to find a curriculum partner. Then you can use the hours in your week to contextualize, customize, and personalize that message for your church. You can use your imaginary conversations to bring someone else's words to life, to make them better, and to help them connect with those you are called to reach.

HAVE IMAGINARY CONVERSATIONS SO . . .
WHAT HAPPENS ON THE PLATFORM WILL PROMPT WHAT HAPPENS IN THE SMALL GROUP.

Some things are communicated better from a platform than in a circle. That's why we think it's so important to structure your ministry in a way where large group environments work as a step to group, as a step to a better experience in group, and as a step to create a culture of groups. But there is also a relational benefit to letting a skilled communicator teach, so your small group leaders don't have to.

Putting the most dynamic, articulate teacher you have on the platform will inevitably improve your small group experiences. But you can take it a step further. Your communicators can leverage their message to prompt what happens in small group. And here are four practical ways to do that:

1. **Start with the small group experience.** Before you write a talk or customize a message, think about what you want to happen in group. Have an imaginary small group conversation. What do you hope they will talk about? When you begin with the end in mind, it will change the way you set up the conversation.

2. **Say what you can say, so they don't have to say it.** Your SGL's primary goal is to give a kid a safe place to process faith. So, when you leverage a master communicator to present truth, you do something remarkable for the group. You give them a leader who is neutral, someone who didn't just teach them something they may want to challenge. As you consider the message, think through what a master communicator can say from the platform so the leader can spend less time wearing a teacher hat, and more time facilitating the conversation.

3. **Set up the tension.** When a communicator explains the idea too thoroughly, answers every possible critique, and makes every possible application, there's very little left to talk about in small group. It seems counterintuitive for most communicators, but it helps the group experience when a communicator can leave a few things unresolved. It's okay to resolve tension when you're communicating to preschoolers, but as kids get older, unresolved tension will become an important tool to keep kids engaged and to set up groups to win.

4. **Say one thing.** There's a limit to what a kid (or adult) can really process in one hour. Small group experiences help kids personalize and apply biblical truth, but that can't happen when they have to spend the first half of group trying to figure out what the message was about. Your message should have one, clear bottom line. The clearer the message, the faster your small groups can get to application.

HAVE IMAGINARY CONVERSATIONS SO . . .
WHAT YOU SAY TO LEADERS DURING THE WEEK WILL GUIDE WHAT THEY SAY TO KIDS DURING SMALL GROUP.

Every leader wants a plan and a script for their group time. Without a script, your leaders might do nothing but talk about the mating habits of wild boar every week, or try to take their third-grade girls through *Mere Christianity*. Being relevant and strategic about your environments means you don't let your leaders run rogue. Instead, you spend a considerable amount of your week evaluating your small group materials.

If you want the application of your message to be experienced in a small group context, then the activities and questions you give your leaders are one of the most critical elements of your weekly curriculum. Effective activities and questions take time and a *lot* of imaginary conversations. Here are just a few things you should keep in mind.

1. **Accommodate a variety of learning styles.** Not every kid processes information in the same way. Some kids learn better by listening, some by talking. Some learn better by watching, some by doing. Since one style won't fit all, your activities should never be weighted too much toward one learning style.

2. **Consider the age of your audience**. A preschooler is very different than a first grader, and the mind of a first grader is not the same as the mind of a third grader. When you evaluate your curriculum, the activities, and questions should change according to the age and stage of the child. If child development isn't your thing, find an educator you trust, someone who understands child development, and have them review your small group curriculum.

3. **Relate to the culture of your demographic**. No curriculum will ever
    be exactly what you need for your context. So, take the material
    through some filters. Are the examples and applications reflective
    of your socioeconomic, ethnic, and regional make-up? How can you
    customize this material to leverage your particular culture for the sake
    of your message?

4. **Rarely give them something that can be answered with one
    word.** Whether the answer is "Yes," "No," "Jesus," or "The Bible,"
    posing a question that can be answered with one word is typically
    a conversation killer. The exception to the one-word answer rule is
    if the question can be answered with a variety of singular words.
    "What's your favorite Olympic sport?" is a one-word question that
    can open a conversation.

5. **Don't confuse a conversation guide with a study guide.** The
    purpose of small group is to help kids process and apply biblical
    truth, not to help kids pass a biblical literacy test. That means
    your small group materials guide conversations. A study guide
    in an open group setting can quickly alienate kids who are less
    adept learners. If every question has a right answer, kids will
    determine for themselves whether they are smart enough or not
    smart enough to belong in church. Please don't miss this: Church
    isn't a place where smart people belong. It's a place where
    everyone belongs.

6. **Ask some questions "just for fun."** Seriously. Groups should be fun.
    If you want kids to come back, and if you want them to enjoy being
    with their leaders and with each other, then they probably need to
    laugh together. If they don't laugh together, they will probably never
    feel comfortable enough to talk with each other about their questions,
    their doubts, or their life experiences. So, give them something fun to
    do and something fun to talk about—every week.

HAVE IMAGINARY CONVERSATIONS SO . . .
**WHAT LEADERS THINK ABOUT *BEFORE* GROUP WILL AFFECT HOW
THEY NAVIGATE THE CONVERSATION *DURING* GROUP.**

As much time as you spend customizing a guide for your small group
leaders this week (and you should), just realize your leaders may not

stick to it (and they shouldn't). If you are empowering great leaders, they will know their few better than you do. Which means they will ultimately be the ones who have the imaginary conversations to contextualize specifically for their particular group.

Just remember, you have an advantage over your SGLs. You are in this full-time, or part-time, so you see the big picture. You understand the scope and cycle of your content. You know where you're headed and why. That's helpful information for the leader who will be navigating conversations in group next week. Every week, you should use every method of communication possible to help your leaders see the big picture. Send them a video. Send them a podcast. Send them a paragraph. Email them personally. Post something to a private leader group. Send them a short text. If you want to help them navigate their group time effectively, you have to help them think about a few things before they get there.

You can help your leaders navigate their group time when you:

1. **Train them to move away from the script.** No leader guide is perfect. There are days when the activities flop, when the topic isn't connecting, or when the night before was Halloween and everyone has a sugar hangover. It happens. Let your leaders know they have your permission to do what they need to do—even if it means going a little off-script.

    "We regularly remind our SGLs not to try to get through every question every week. We want them to feel comfortable leaving some questions unanswered, or even unasked. We have to trust our leaders and empower them to decide what is effective for their own group or what isn't." – **Adam Duckworth** *(Elementary)*

    "One day during small group time, I saw one of our leaders doing jumping jacks with his group of third graders in the hallway! They were jumping and saying the words to their memory verse. The leader looked 'caught' and apologized as he explained to me that his group always has a lot of extra energy and he was trying to find ways to engage them. I told him it was brilliant! I was so glad he felt the freedom to improvise, letting those boys put their energy to work." – **Bobbi Miller** *(Elementary)*

"Whenever our group got stuck, and the questions weren't working we would resume our great small group debate: 'Who would win in a fight: a bear or a gorilla?' It might not have given a lot of spiritual insight, but for my tenth-grade guys it let them connect and kept our group fun instead of letting things get awkward."
– **Matt Ivy** (High School)

2. **Give them a clear destination.** If your leaders are going to go off-script, they need to know where they are headed. When you're in week one of a series, let them know the bottom lines for week two and three so they won't accidently cover next week's idea this week and regret it later. Give them a clear goal for their conversation this week so that even if they don't follow the plan and the script, they know what a win looks like.

3. **Alert them to foreseeable challenges.** When you are covering a story about Lazarus with Kindergartners, kids may have questions about death. When you talk about miracles with third graders, they may ask you about their sick grandmother. When you talk about respect for authority with students, there may be some who present some challenging scenarios. If you are covering a topic that's likely to raise some challenging questions, give your leaders a heads up. It's always easier to navigate when you aren't caught off-guard.

→ When you get in the habit of having imaginary conversations before group, you cooperate with what is already happening so groups happen better.

CONTROL
THE CLIMATE

(Let's talk about your **context**.)

Okay, no one can really control the climate. And no ministry leader can fully control the experience every kid has in small group. But there are external factors you can control as a staff member that affect the quality of the group experience. These are the factors that make up your physical space.

As you create a culture in your ministry where every kid has a place to belong, don't make the mistake of under-thinking your physical space. Relationships may be what connect them to your ministry, but what you do with your physical spaces can support those relational connections or undermine them.

If you don't believe me, think about
American Girl
Legoland
Starbucks
Disney

A few months ago, I (Kristen) had one of the most magical days of my life. I say magical because at thirty-two years old, I finally experienced my first day at the Magic Kingdom. Growing up I never went to any Disney park, so this was literally the experience of a lifetime. I paid one lady one time, and she handed me a Mickey bracelet and a pin with confetti on it to celebrate my first Disney experience. I never had to pay again. Any time I wanted anything, I just bumped the Mickey bracelet and I had it— like Magic. When I entered the park and turned down Main Street I was greeted by a parade of people dancing and singing and celebrating me and my big day. When I met the Mouse himself, he spoke to me as if the living, breathing, cartoon character had stepped out of the Big Screen just to welcome me. He even complimented my seven-year-old companion on her beautiful Elsa dress. We used a Fast Pass to avoid lines. We experienced cool mist blown onto us out of thin air when the day warmed up. The ambient music changed subtly as we moved from Tomorrowland to Adventureland to Fantasyland. I never saw a single piece of trash or anyone carrying out the trash.

WHAT WAS UNBELIEVABLY REMARKABLE ABOUT MY TRIP TO DISNEY IS THIS: I HAD WAITED FOR THIS DAY FOR THIRTY-TWO YEARS AND THEY WELCOMED ME WHEN I ARRIVED AS IF THEY HAD BEEN ANTICIPATING MY ARRIVAL WITH AS MUCH EXPECTANCY AS I HAD.

We have a few friends who work for Disney parks, and in spite of what it felt like to experience the park, I know what I experienced wasn't actually magic. It's the result of a lot of hard work and deliberation. With an average of 46,000 visitors per day, even the Magic Kingdom has to be strategic about how to dispose of trash in a way that isn't intrusive—the fairy dust doesn't really just blow it all away.

Memories can be made in any environment, but there are some environments that foster connection in a better way because someone has taken the time to control the climate.

You may not be starting with the most attractive or practical physical space. You probably don't have the budget of Disney parks. The space may not even be your own if you are in a mobile or multipurpose environment. But there are things you can control that will let every guest know you were thinking about them before they got there, and you care about the experience they have while they are with you.

Before we move into some of the characteristics of an environment that supports relational connections, it's important to make this one observation. **You don't see your physical space the same way a first time guest sees it.** When you live somewhere for too long, when you work somewhere too often, there are things you stop noticing. They become part of the unseen backdrop of your life.

There were actually a few times I (Reggie) paid high school kids in our community to come sit in our weekly environment for teenagers. I wasn't trying to manipulate our numbers. I wanted to hear their perspective. What was the experience like for them? Was there anything about the experience that was off-putting or "weird"? We also know some leaders who church-swap by inviting a neighboring pastor to come to their environment—not to show it off, but to help each other see what the other no longer sees.

For the next few pages, we thought we'd identify a few characteristics of spaces that work best when it comes to creating environments where every kid knows they belong.

CONTROL THE CLIMATE SO . . .
YOUR PHYSICAL SPACE WELCOMES EVERYONE.

Sometimes I wonder what could happen in any environment if the people in charge began to act like today was their customer's first experience with them. My first visit to Disney wasn't the first time Mickey greeted a guest. It wasn't the first time the characters paraded down Main Street. And it wasn't the first time Cinderella talked to a raving adult fan. But they made it feel as if it were. They greeted us, welcomed us, and directed us so there was never an awkward or out-of-place moment.

If you want kids to know they belong when they are in group, make sure they feel like they belong before they get to group.

From the moment a kid or their parent drives onto your property, every guest should know where they are supposed to go. As soon as they enter your physical space, let them know you have been expecting them. If you have a parking lot, how are you welcoming them and showing them where to enter the building? If you live in a walking city, who stands at your door to greet them when they walk in? You can position volunteers to greet and welcome guests every step of the way. And you can control how those volunteers make a kid feel.

If they don't know where to go, they won't feel like they belong.

CONTROL THE CLIMATE SO . . .
YOUR PHYSICAL SPACE APPEALS TO YOUR AUDIENCE.

When you invite guests to your home, what do you do? You clean up. You organize the clutter, you sweep the floor, you light a candle. If they are staying overnight, you change the sheets, lay out clean towels, and make sure to have food and drinks on hand. When you know someone is coming over, you let them know you were thinking about them before they got there.

If you are expecting guests to show up at your church, you should behave the same way. Maybe don't lay out clean towels, because that would be weird. But make your physical spaces appealing.

If hosting has never come naturally to you, here's a practical tip. Each week, have someone walk through your environments and play the sense game. Ask these questions:

> What does it sound like?
> What does it smell like?
> What does it look like?
> What does it feel like?

You might not be able to control some of the smells in your environments after they arrive, but you can start things off right—and you can keep a can of Lysol handy. The temperature, the lighting, the seating, and the décor all matter when it comes to making kids feel at ease in your church.

Small group environments can be challenging—especially when you are creating them in shared spaces. Just remember, what works for adults probably doesn't work for second graders. And what works for preschoolers won't translate well for high school juniors. If you've ever walked through Pottery Barn Kids or Pottery Barn Teen it's obvious someone in that organization understands different ages. What's impressive is how they take a large open store-front space and create sectioned-off, age-specific environments that let you feel as if you've stepped right into the world of a fourth-grade boy.

In the same way, when you create small group spaces for kids and teenagers, keep your target audience in mind. Whether you have a traditional church facility, a mobile set-up, a large auditorium or a movie theatre, section your spaces off to give them a place of their own.

❝

"For preschoolers, we have tables and chairs for small groups because of the hands-on nature of some of the activities. But for Kindergarten and first grade we use carpet circles." – **Adam Duckworth** (Elementary)

"The best small group we ever had with Kindergartners was when we met in the chapel. The pews and the stained glass made us all feel reverent and it kept us focused." – **no small group leader ever**

"Circle rugs have gone a long way toward defining the amount of space a group has and reminding them of the value of small. When a group decides to combine, it is a constant visual reminder that the group is too big." – **Gina McClain** (Elementary)

"I believe in private meeting places for groups in middle school. They need to feel safe. It doesn't have to be a room, per se, but it needs to be a place where you don't have to worry about people listening. We convert our church offices to middle school small group rooms so it's a good stewardship of space." – **Tom Shefchunas** (Middle School)

Some ministries have high school groups that meet Sunday evening or mid-week in order to provide them with optimal spaces. Some ministries convert large rooms so they are more conducive to small group focus. Some ministries move their small groups off-site. The goal is all the same. Give them a place they can call their own. And give them a space that appeals specifically to them.

CONTROL THE CLIMATE SO . . .
YOUR PHYSICAL SPACE COMMUNICATES YOUR MESSAGE.

When I (Kristen) was a high school teacher, one of my favorite things was rearranging my room. Maybe it's because any change is a good change when your room is four square walls of cinderblock with fluorescent lighting and concrete floors. But I simply loved setting the stage for what was going to happen. I wanted students to walk through the doors with an expectation that something could happen in the room that was more than what the classroom shell conveyed. On test days it was a classroom, but when we started a unit on suspense the lights were off, electric candles were lit, and creepy music played on the boom box from the corner. (Yep. It had a tape deck.) When we studied *Lord of the Flies*, they walked in to the theme music for *Lost* and the desks were arranged by "island." When we had debate conversations, the desks were arranged in one large inner circle and one large outer circle.

No matter how simple or complex your physical space and no matter how mobile your environments, you can use your space to communicate your message.

"We use music, stage decor, props, signage, fun on-screen graphics, and every other resource we can think of to communicate our message by engaging all the senses." – **Amy Fenton** (Elementary)

Using your physical spaces to communicate your message doesn't mean your spaces have to be elaborate. In fact, sometimes a simpler physical space can work to your advantage. We have a friend who inherited a jungle. Literally. It was a fun-looking space, but the problem was they weren't talking about jungles every week, and over time the jungle began to compete with their weekly message. The context of your environment should complement the content, not distract

In the same way, if your space stays the same for too long, whatever your messaging is, it will get lost. It can become white noise. But when you intentionally rearrange your space and change out elements of the design, your physical space can enhance the weekly message in a fresh new way.

How does this apply to small groups? Think about all the ways you can customize your space so kids and teenagers can visually see what you want to communicate. What are you putting on your walls to help kids remember the bottom line? What are you putting in the hallways and throughout your physical spaces that will make your message stick?

CONTROL THE CLIMATE SO . . .
YOUR PHYSICAL SPACE EQUIPS YOUR LEADERS.

If you've led ministry for over a week, you know this: your volunteers need resources to be successful. They need Bibles. They need activity supplies. They need conversation guides. But if you're creating a lead small culture, you will be especially concerned with how your environments provide the resources your small group leaders need.

As children's directors, Adam Duckworth and Gina McClain both talk about reorganizing the way they resource leaders so they can reinforce their belief in small groups. They both transitioned from a system of "curriculum carts" (holding enough supplies for an entire grade level), to a cart holding individual tubs of supplies with just enough materials for each small group.

> *"It made a huge difference in how our the SGLs viewed their group."*
> – **Adam Duckworth** and **Gina McClain** (Elementary)

How can a quote be by two people? They literally share the same story. Different churches, different contexts, but they both drew the same conclusion. Funny how that happens.

I (Elle) use a similar approach when prepping our middle school environments. Our groups do fewer activities, but we know there will be weeks when leaders want to mix things up and try something new. When that happens, we want to give them everything they need to be as creative as they want to be. So, we plan for the unknown. We give them Bibles, blank paper, pens, post cards, the occasional group activity, and card games that encourage conversation. Oh, and we give them candy. Because we feel like the best way to a middle schooler's heart is through a good sugar rush.

When your physical space equips your leaders, they are free to focus on their few. They know they can create an experience in their group because they trust they will have whatever they need on hand to make that happen. When you use your space to resource your leaders, you control the climate and foster an environment where groups can win.

CONTROL THE CLIMATE SO . . .
YOUR PHYSICAL SPACE IS SAFE.

Educational theorists have written about this for years; physical needs precede our ability to process emotionally and intellectually. If you want small groups to work, the kids in your groups need to feel safe. So, make sure your physical spaces actually *are* safe. If they aren't safe, very little else will matter. You've probably already thought of this, which is why you probably have already done most of the things on this list. That's great! Consider it a list to show others how much you are already doing.

1. **Run background checks.** Background checks aren't one hundred percent preventative, but they are an important guard to put in place to help your environment stay safe.

2. **Have a check-in system and a bathroom policy**. Never leave a kid alone without an adult. Never leave a kid alone with only one adult. Have automated systems and policies to ensure every kid is accounted for.

3. **Eliminate the obvious hazards.** Kids will get hurt and kids will break stuff. Some things are inevitable, but every week you should run a basic safety check to avoid the dangers and liabilities that are avoidable. Are the outlets in your toddler spaces covered? Are the scissors in your elementary spaces put away? Have you removed the clay chalice your executive pastor brought back from the Holy Land from the table in your eighth-grade guys small group room?

4. **Control the entrances, the exits, and the alleys**. We aren't saying you create environments as unassailable as Alcatraz. But while kids and teenagers are with you, you have a responsibility to make sure they don't leave and no one leaves with them. If you work with students, remember being seventeen. If you leave the pews unmonitored, someone will make out in them. And when Melissa's mom picks her up from your ministry with a hickey that wasn't there when she dropped her off, you will answer for it. Don't let Melissa get a hickey during student ministry. Monitor your hallways.

You don't have to create a bracelet with a chip in it to monitor the movements of every child, but you would be surprised at what soap, paint, a piece of round carpet, and working air conditioning can actually do for your space. Controlling your environment may begin with some basics.

A few years ago we went to a church in southern California with a student building that was separate from the rest of the church. Since it was in SoCal, the temperatures were fairly moderate, which is why the deacons of the church weren't overly concerned that the student space didn't have centralized air. The youth pastor put in a budget request several years in a row. After being continually denied, he did something creative. He scheduled space in the main building during the deacons meeting and had the deacons meet in the student space in mid-July. The next year when he put in a request for AC, it was approved.

Whatever improvements you want to make in your physical spaces, begin with baby steps. You won't have the budget or the volunteer staff to get there overnight. So, start small. Make incremental changes. Control the climate every week so your physical space . . .
welcomes everyone.
appeals to your audience.
communicates the message.
equips your leaders.
is safe.

→ When you get in the habit of controlling the climate of your ministry, you will create a context where what you say can actually be heard.

MEASURE WHAT SEEMS UNMEASURABLE

(Let's talk about your **connections**.)

Some things in life are easy to measure.

How many times did you tweet?
How many Double Stuf Oreos did you eat?
How many miles per gallon does your vehicle get?

Some things in life are harder to measure.

How much water is in the ocean?
How many people live in the Ukraine?
How much milk can a seventh grader drink without puking?

Then there are some things that seem unmeasurable.

How much does a mother love her child?
How do you know when someone is "over" their ex?
How well does a foster child integrate into a new home?

When it comes to the things that seem unmeasurable, you notice a common element: relational connections. People don't have high-tech digital monitors to indicate how connected they feel. There isn't a "mood ring" or a hyper-color T-shirt (remember those?) to let you know if every kid feels like your ministry is a place where they belong. Wouldn't it be great if there were?

EVEN THOUGH YOU CAN'T VISUALLY, TANGIBLY MEASURE THE DEPTH OF A RELATIONSHIP OR THE DEGREE TO WHICH SOMEONE IS CONNECTED, YOU CAN OBSERVE A FEW THINGS THAT WILL INDICATE WHETHER OR NOT A KID FEELS KNOWN.

The most basic indicator is something pretty profound:
A kid will feel known when someone knows them.

A kid will feel known when someone knows them.

Seriously. When there is a consistent leader who knows their name, their dog's name, and the way they like to fix their hot dog with relish and cheese and no mustard, then a kid will feel known. And there's a good chance kids need to feel known by someone before they will feel known and loved by God.

Have you ever thought about the fact that there's a connection between knowing and caring?

Maybe that's why the Psalmist wrote about God's intricate knowledge of creation.

He determines the number of the stars and calls them each by name. Great is our Lord and mighty in power; His understanding has no limit.
Psalm 147:4-5

Or why there is an entire Psalm dedicated to God's knowledge of us.

You have searched me, Lord, and you know me. You know when I sit and when I rise; you perceive my thoughts from afar. You discern my going out and my lying down; you are familiar with all my ways. Before a word is on my tongue you, Lord, know it completely. You hem me in behind and before, and you lay your hand upon me.
Psalm 139:1-5

Or why Luke reminds us that God knows the very number of hairs on our head.

That's a pretty strange thing to know when you really think about it. Why hairs on our head? It seems like a random thing to mention. But we think the purpose is simple: God wants us to know how much He knows, because it shows how much He cares.

If you want to measure the success of your weekly experiences, you should ask two questions.

Are kids connected?
Are they known?

That may seem like an over-simplification. But, remember you can't measure something until you've taken the time to define what really matters. When it comes to creating a culture of small groups, your goal is to give a kid a person and a place so they will know they belong. So, your measurements should be designed to evaluate how well you are succeeding at that goal.

And you do need measurements.

Just like . . .
a poet knows words.
a mathematician knows formulas.
Elle knows sloth YouTube videos.
you actually need to know some details about your ministry.

Knowing shows you care—and it may actually make you care more.

If you are not wired for structure, it may not come naturally for you to focus on details and numbers and reporting. But there are some details that matter too much to be ignored, which is why someone in your ministry should know the details. Someone should own the weekly job of evaluating your ministry to see if connection is happening.

If you're still not big on trying to measure the unmeasurable, maybe this is something to consider. You might as well evaluate what you do. Chances are someone else is already looking over your shoulder to gauge how well they think your ministry is working.

Maybe it's a senior or executive pastor.
Maybe it's the parents.
Maybe it's the kids or teenagers.

Here's a question. Who decides which yardsticks should be used to measure what you do? If you aren't a part of clarifying the win for your ministry, someone else will be. If you aren't proactively evaluating your ministry, others will evaluate it for you. And if someone is evaluating you by a different standard, you can imagine how well your ministry will measure up: kind of like NFL quarterback RG3 competing on *Iron Chef America*.

Don't let an outsider evaluate your ministry for you. Determine what the win looks like as a team, then proactively evaluate your weekly experiences. Let everyone agree on the standard you're using to measure success, then invite them to give you feedback.

JUST REMEMBER: THERE WILL STILL BE TIMES YOUR MINISTRY WILL FEEL UNMEASURABLE. THAT'S BECAUSE YOU CAN'T MEASURE WHAT'S HAPPENING IN THE MIND OF A KID. YOU CAN'T MEASURE WHAT'S HAPPENING SPIRITUALLY IN THEIR LIFE. YOU CAN'T MEASURE WHAT THEY ARE FEELING EMOTIONALLY.

But there are some things every ministry *can* do to measure connection.

YOU MEASURE THE UNMEASURABLE WHEN YOU . . .
COUNT THE NUMBERS.

I know what you're thinking, *This isn't about numbers.* Well, maybe in some ways it is. Numbers will never tell the whole story. But they will always tell part of it if you know how to interpret them. You can't quantify spiritual growth. But you can look to the numbers as an indicator of some things. Maybe it helps to think of your ministry numbers like the scores in gymnastics.

When you're watching gymnastics on television and the judges flash what seems like an arbitrary number on the scoreboard, it's easy to think to yourself, *That's subjective.* But the scores aren't arbitrary. They are guided by clear and consistent guidelines. Every skill has an optimum value and every error made deducts from that total. Are the judges perfect? No. Will the score capture the essence of the performance? No. But the number the judges give for each routine will quantify something about the skill level and performance so it can be evaluated in comparison with another.

Remember, it's hard to manage what you can't measure. It's hard to improve your weekly experiences if you don't have a system of evaluation.

There are a few things you can measure quantitatively when it comes to your weekly experiences:

How often do kids come back?   Are they inviting friends?   Are new baptisms taking place?   Is your attendance up or down?

As you track these numbers, you are the interpreter of the data. Work with your team to interpret what they mean. If numbers are up, is there a reason you think it happened? If numbers are down, is there an explanation for why you think the drop is occurring? What do you know about the demographic of your community that informs your interpretation of data? Because if you lead a church in Chandler, Arizona, your numbers may be down in early March simply because it's hard to compete with the live ostrich race happening right outside your doors.

YOU MEASURE THE UNMEASURABLE WHEN YOU . . .
READ THE CROWD.

A skilled communicator on the platform can read the room. He or she can tell when the audience is leaning in, or when their attention is waning. As a communicator reads the room, they make adjustments to help their message connect with their audience. In the same way, you can read the connections in your ministry. But unlike a communicator, the information you need isn't sitting in front of you. You have to first identify who your audience is.

You have three crowds to read on a consistent basis:

Kids or Students
You're probably already reading the crowd when it comes to your most immediate audience. As you read them to see if they are connecting, you might ask yourself some of these questions:
Who do they talk about?
Who are they introducing their friends to?
Are they tweeting, posting, and talking about what happens in group?

The more you create a culture where kids belong in group, the more you will hear them talk about their group experience. So, look for ways they are showing or not showing signs of that connection.

"I have a group of students that are my 'ears in the streets.' I ask them how are things going and how other students are responding. I task my student leaders to help keep me informed on how our students are connecting, engaging, and growing spiritually." – **Jeff Wallace** (High School)

Parents

Parents are paying attention to what happens with their kid or teenager when they are with you. You probably don't need us to tell you that. You get their emails. But your parents aren't simply your raving fans or your harshest critics. They can be one of the greatest indicators of whether or not you are creating a culture where kids know they belong.

When it comes to parents, here are some questions to ask to help you read your audience:

Do parents know the name and contact information of their kid's SGL? Do parents see the SGL as a partner? Do they connect with the SGL directly? What do parents celebrate about your ministry, and what frustrates them?

"We are always listening to parents and their feedback. It's one of the keys to our ability to evaluate our ministry. They know when their kids are not connecting. Sometimes it's an indication of a personality issue and we need to re-assign a particular kid. Sometimes it's a red flag that life-change isn't happening in a group as a whole and something bigger needs to change." – **Amy Fenton** (Elementary)

Small Group Leaders

If you are giving ministry away to leaders, you should be reading the leaders to see if connection is really happening. As you listen to the leaders, pay attention to what they are frustrated about. They *will* be frustrated. A successful lead small culture won't mean you have eliminated the frustrations of all your leaders. It will mean you have shifted to a culture where your leaders are frustrated by the same things that frustrate you.

When you create a culture where every leader understands their role to connect with kids, they will be

> MORE FRUSTRATED BY. . .

- not having enough time to connect.
- kids who can't find a ride.
- noise that distracts when a kid wants to share a story.

< LESS FRUSTRATED BY. . .

- a disruptive child who talks when they are talking.
- games that take time away from the lesson.
- not having enough chairs for the classroom.

Beyond their frustrations, listen to the stories they celebrate. What are they saying and what are they not saying?

Life is messy. When you create a system of relational ministry, you should expect some messy stuff. When kids have an adult who has given them a safe place, they are likely to share some things that will have you putting a licensed counselor on speed dial. If nothing messy is coming up, it may be an indicator that you still have a way to go to make the kids in your ministry feel like they have a safe place.

I (Elle) have been working for several years to create a culture in our middle school ministry where small groups are the answer. It has taken time, and we are still constantly working on it, but one of the greatest moments for me happened at our staff-facilitated Coffee Talks. We posed strategic questions to our SGLs and then let them talk with each other. They began to look to each other for suggestions on small group activities and ways to reach out to parents. They asked each other how to handle disruptive situations in group and shared best practices. Our staff just sat back and learned from them. That was when I knew we had created a "culture" because we could watch it course-correct.

YOU MEASURE THE UNMEASURABLE WHEN YOU . . .
ASK KEY QUESTIONS.

If reading the crowd is how you observe the culture around you, asking questions is like taking the official census. There are some things you may not ever hear if you are simply being intentional about listening to what leaders are saying on their own—unprompted. You need regularly scheduled times to ask your leaders some key questions.

Some questions are benchmarks.
You have asked your SGLs to take on a pretty significant role in a kid's life, so it only makes sense that you would follow up with them to see how kids are connecting. If the success of your ministry is connected to their success in group, you should be asking things like:

> Are the kids on your roster showing up?
> Who has stopped coming?
> Who are you having trouble connecting with?

It's not realistic for every SGL to connect with every kid you put on their roster. But they may be your best resource for identifying anyone who is getting lost and coming up with a better plan to connect them.

Whatever expectations you have set out for your SGLs, don't be afraid to ask them how it's going. Evaluating their success is a part of how you evaluate your success as a ministry.

Some questions prompt stories.
Some SGLs share their stories unprompted; others may need for you to ask some questions to prompt their stories. So, when you connect with your SGLs weekly to ask for specific feedback, remember to ask questions that will lead to stories. Questions like:

What's the best thing that happened in your group lately?
What do you have coming up in your group that you're excited about?

"We ask questions to glean stories from SGLs and listen for those connections. I frequently ask leaders what their kids are requesting prayer for. By asking the question, I know I'm reminding my leaders of the priority of prayer time, and I'm also gaining insight into the leaders' connection with their few." – **Gina McClain** (Elementary)

Some questions generate feedback.
As you evaluate your SGLs, your SGLs are evaluating you. They have insights about your ministry. So, when and where are you giving them an opportunity to share their thoughts with you? When you meet with your SGLs weekly, ask questions to invite their input. Questions like:

Do you have the resources you need for group time?
Are you able to fill the time you have every week, or are you constantly running out of time?
What's one thing that would help make your group experience better?

In his ministry in Georgia, Jeff Wallace created a system for getting strategic input from his leaders. "We have quarterly 'creative team' meetings to go over every aspect of our weekly programming and small group questions. In our creative team meetings, we deal with the good, the bad, and the ugly of the previous series and then we begin to break down the questions for the up-and-coming series and make sure they are relevant to the climate of the current culture. We have a representative leader from middle school, high school, worship and arts, as well as a few older high school students that make up this team."

Then there's one more question you should ask every SGL every time you meet. It's pretty simple, but incredibly powerful.

HOW CAN I HELP?

SGLs need permission to ask for help when they need it. If you ask them regularly how you can help, you train them to know it's okay for them to come to you for assistance. Their answers to this question will help you know more about what's working and what's not working as you measure the experience that happens in groups.

When you meet with SGLs to measure the unmeasurable, remind them that this is a long-term investment. You are on the same team. Collectively, you are thinking beyond today. There will be some weekly experiences that SGLs and kids will talk about years later, and there will be some experiences that seem to make very little impact.

"Don't expect 'a moment' to happen every week. If they connect, that's a moment." – **Sue Miller** (Preschool/Elementary)

As important as measuring and improving your ministry is, you'll never measure everything in ministry. There will always be things happening that you can't see. And if you can't see it, you can't measure it. In 1 Corinthians, Paul explains an important principle about discipleship with a farming analogy. I'm not sure if you've ever grown anything, but it must have worked in that context.

I planted the seed, Apollos watered it, but God has been making it grow. So neither the one who plants nor the one who waters is anything, but only God, who makes things grow. The one who plants and the one who waters have one purpose, and they will each be rewarded according to their own labor. For we are co-workers in God's service; you are God's field, God's building. **1 Corinthians 3:6-9**

The successes of your ministry aren't yours alone. There are others who have gone before you to love and influence the kids and teenagers you serve. There will be others after you who will continue to influence those who passed through the doors of your ministry. Your ministry will produce results that *you* will never see, but someone down the road may see them. That's why you can't give up. You have to keep being faithful with the time and influence you have. You measure what seems unmeasurable because there is too much at stake. The job you've been called to do matters.

And remember, it's "God who makes things grow," not you. God is at work in the lives of kids. You can plan and execute and measure and improve, but you also need to trust. Trust that there is more happening than what you can see, and more to your investment than you can really measure. Trust that God is up to something bigger and greater than you can imagine.

→ When you get in the habit of measuring the unmeasurable, you significantly increase your chances of making sure every kid feels known.

CONCERT
CLASSROOM
CIRCLES

DO MORE THAN A CONCERT

Some of you are already implementing a small group strategy. We hope this book has reinforced much of what you already know and has given you some tangible ways to improve. Others of you are still in transition. You may be holding on to the positive things that have existed in your church's tradition, while at the same time trying to reinvent your ministry to be more relevant to the needs of a changing culture. (That's just another way of saying you are trying to change things without making someone mad.)

So, let's talk about change.

If you are going to transition something, it's important to know where you are and where you want to go. We have a friend who always says, "You're not transitioning if you don't know what you are transitioning to." That's why we think it's critical to discuss a few other basic approaches related to how some churches do children and student ministry.

We typically don't think labels are fair. Primarily, they're not fair because they tend to narrowly define a model or approach in a way that doesn't adequately represent all the facts. So, when we use a term to describe a model, it's not an attempt to attach a label but to identify certain characteristics of one approach so we can clarify the potential differences in another approach. That being said, let's take a look at one model that has been traditionally used to minister to kids and teenagers.

The Concert Model
The concert model is focused on gathering the maximum number of kids in a room and making an engaging presentation. We use the word *concert* because of the similarity it has to a rock concert. It draws a crowd. It usually involves a level of production, is personality-driven and has a band. The concert model for kids usually attempts to be a "more hip" version of what is happening in adult "big church." Many churches have traditionally built large rooms where they can do children's church and youth services, complete with age-appropriate music and teaching.

I (Reggie) was actually groomed as a student pastor in the concert model, along with a host of my friends in ministry. Some of us who started

North Point even joke that one of the secrets to our growth is that we just kept doing student ministry for the adults who grew up. The concert model is an effective way to craft your skill as a speaker and to engage a crowd of people to worship corporately. If it is done strategically and with excellence, it provides a front door to engage people with core truths of the Christian faith and to connect people to the church. Through the years, I have been aware of thousands of kids and teenagers who were influenced to trust Christ and become engaged in ministry because of effective weekly gatherings like these.

The appeal of the concert model is that . . .
it's the fastest way to communicate to the most kids or students.
it only needs a limited amount of volunteers.
it's typically easy to measure and manage.

In a concert model, it is fairly obvious when things are working. People . . .
laugh,
applaud,
talk back to you,
tweet what you say,
smile,
and in some cases even go to an altar.
(Try explaining an altar to un-churched parents sometime.)

If teenagers enjoy it, they will come back. Most children have to come back whether they like it or not because their parents make them. But when it comes to the concert model . . .
you can count the seats and know how many attend.
you can monitor the quality of the production.
you can usually know if it is working.

The primary limitation to the concert model is when it ends, kids leave. And at that point no one is really connected to anything, except the experience. The goal is to make that experience as engaging as possible so kids will come back every week.

The other thing to realize about the concert model is that it typically has a lot of competition outside the church. It is difficult for churches to produce a quality experience that can measure up to what's happening in culture.

You may have that deacon in your church who knows how to juggle, but Disney has Mickey.

You may have the teenager who almost made it through the first round of *American Idol*, but next Sunday Justin is doing a concert in town. (And I'm not talking Bieber.)

I have worked with churches that have invested thousands or hundreds of thousands of dollars in creating unique concert-type experiences. I have seen some pretty amazing productions designed for kids and teenagers. (We already wrote about why we think every church should do its best to create excellent environments.) But so far I haven't seen any church consistently out-produce Disney, MTV, Nickelodeon, or put on a show like Barry Manilow—uh . . . I mean, JT. The sobering truth is that regardless of how much money your church spends, it will never really consistently compete with what most million-dollar entertainment entities can produce.

Please carefully consider this next point.
Although the average church can never compete with what culture can produce, culture can never compete with what the average church can do in the life of a kid.

To state it another way, whenever the church gives kids a safe place to belong with people who believe in them, it does something nothing else in culture can do. Loving people unconditionally is a unique contribution the church can make. Regardless of your location, size, or budget, you are called, gifted, and empowered by the Holy Spirit to connect with and care for people. When you fulfill that calling, you are doing something no other entity can match. Why wouldn't you learn to play to your strength as a church? Recognize that while you may have limited resources and need to economize financially, it's vital *not* to economize in the one area of your ministry with the most potential. Prioritize for relationships.

Another limitation of the concert model is the capacity of the personality on stage. We've talked a lot about capacity, but that's because we think it matters. It's critical to embrace the idea of building a healthy relational model around more than one personality. Ironically, the very personality at the center of making the concert model successful also has the potential to determine if a small group model is successful.

For more than a decade, I was fortunate enough to work next to a lead pastor, Andy Stanley, who strategically managed the tension between the concert model and small groups. On one hand, our church recognized

Although the average church can never compete with what culture can produce, culture can never compete with what the average church can do in the life of a kid.

the giftedness of a unique communicator who could inspire thousands, and we built the right facilities to create a front door to welcome the community into our church. On the other hand, that same leader was committed to making small groups the priority. He built a team that was always quick to champion and fund a relational ministry to kids and teenagers.

We are not suggesting a concert model is wrong.
We are boldly stating it is not enough.

If you have a ministry designed around a concert model, you need to consider making some adjustments. If you have a concert model that exists alone, without a clear intentional strategy to move people into relationships, it can be dangerous. The concert should primarily exist to get people into circles where they can connect with others.

We have numerous conversations every week with churches that built their children or student ministries around a concert approach. Some of those churches are picking up the pieces of an unhealthy ministry because someone left, and all the fans of that individual followed or quit. Some are in a power struggle between a ministry leader who has built a platform and other leaders who are trying to refocus the ministry relationally.

When you are trying to transition to a relational model, you need to be aware of the potential tensions that can exist between concerts and circles.

Whenever a concert is the primary focus of a ministry . . .
it can make you feel like you are more or less successful than you may actually be.
it can require so much energy or budget that small groups can't win.
it can encourage stage personalities who resist giving others influence.

SO, IF YOU WANT TO BE SUCCESSFUL AT IMPLEMENTING A LEAD SMALL CULTURE . . .

| you have to avoid letting concerts overshadow what happens in your circles. | you have to groom leaders on stage to be more interested in what happens in circles. | you have to allow your concerts to be influenced by those in charge of circles. |

Sure, concerts can be fun and exciting.
Concerts can be amazing experiences.
Concerts can be effective at inspiring a lot of people.

But just remember:
When the music stops,
and the emotion has faded,
and the lights are turned out,
and the doors have been closed,
It's what happens in a small group afterward that really lasts.
You will never disciple kids in a crowd.

DROP OUT OF CLASS

Now, let's jump into another model of ministry churches have promoted over the last several decades. If Sunday is the optimal day to get families to come to church, then it makes sense that Sunday is the most strategic time to teach kids the Bible. It's no wonder churches have traditionally reserved a segment of time on Sunday morning to do just that.

The Classroom Model
The classroom model, or what some people may refer to as Sunday school, was initially designed to teach kids the Bible every Sunday morning. For years, I (Reggie) promoted and built Sunday school programs in a number of churches. My experience convinced me that Sunday school was uniquely designed to teach and educate a child. In my denomination, Sunday school was usually under the direction of a "Minister of Education." (That's not to be confused with government leaders who determine the education policies in a number of countries. Although, the Minister of Education in our church did function like a Vice President to the Senior Pastor.)

The education strategy was simple.
Every age group had a class.
The curriculum was designed to teach the Bible in a systematic way.
Individuals were arranged in classrooms with a teacher who presented a weekly lesson.
Nobody could become a member until they attended three consecutive weeks.
And everyone was evaluated by a weekly report.
(Cleverly designed envelopes recorded attendance, tithe, Bible reading, etc.)

The plan was to design an hour each week to make sure kids who grew up in church were biblically literate. (As we have already stated, the average kid who consistently attends church goes about 40 hours a year. When you contrast that with the 400 hours this year those same kids will study math, reading, or history, you realize it's quite a challenge.)

We created the following chart to illustrate the primary characteristics of a classroom model.

SUNDAY SCHOOL

Goal: **Education**
(That's why Sunday school was directed by a Minister of Education.)

Focus: **Teach the Bible**
(Kids lost points or were called out if they didn't bring one.)

Model: **Classroom**
(That's why teachers referred to it as "my class.")

Time: **Sunday Morning**
(That's why it was called "Sunday" school.)

Priority: **Present the Lesson**
(It was often read, unless someone creative used a flannel board.)

Volunteers: **Recruit Teachers**
(They were the most crucial and celebrated volunteers in ministry.)

Evaluation: **Church Practices**
(Leaders record each child's weekly attendance, Bible reading, tithe, etc.)

Emphasis: **Learning Scripture**
(It involved lots of Bible quizzes, Bible drills, and memory verse games.)

Before I continue, I want to acknowledge that a lot of people owe their faith to committed Sunday school teachers who taught them weekly Bible stories. It has been a meaningful tradition within some denominations for over a century. I am personally convinced that in the past, it had an important role in shaping someone's understanding of the Bible. It worked at a time when families spent most of their day working together, and local communities were characterized by common faith and values.

The truth is: **I'm a Sunday school dropout**. I hate to admit it, but I never enjoyed traditional Sunday school. When I went to church as a kid with my family, I would pretend to go to my class and then sneak back outside to hide in the car until Sunday school was over. Maybe that's why I've actually spent most of my life trying to help leaders stop doing Sunday school. (Or at least to discontinue a style of Sunday school where kids sit in a room and listen to someone teach a lesson.)

We could go into some detail here on the history of Sunday school, and how it was originally started in the late 1700s in England, to educate children who had to work in factories six days a week. But beyond that historical tradition, many leaders believe this model is not the best way to disciple kids. Besides, shouldn't the name "Sunday school" bother us a little? Do we really think kids love school so much they want to go there on Sunday, too?

Many churches are recognizing the need to shift away from the idea of traditional Sunday school. Many ministries have decided to embrace a more relational model, while other churches are still wrestling with how to redefine Sunday school. In some cases they just change the name, but keep following a model that is losing ground.

One of the problems is simply that too many churches still expect a generation to embrace an outdated idea. If you Google "Sunday school," you will still find leaders who are defending and championing the concept as if the model is actually found in the book of Acts. Even those leaders will usually admit that the influence of Sunday school has been steadily declining for decades.

So, what if there isn't going to be a Sunday school revival? What if you can do **something better** than Sunday school? What if it's just time to let go and move on?

Photography is one of my hobbies, and I know a bunch of photographers who lost their business several years ago because they refused to go digital. Why? Because they loved film. Is anything wrong with film? Not at all! Photos made from film have a unique character and beauty unmatched by the average digital image. There will always be those who are advocates for film and may even become famous because of their work with film. But most photographers will not stay with film for one simple reason: People want digital images. They don't use film, and they keep very few prints. This generation uses smartphones to take pics. So, most professionals are competing with people who carry a camera in their pocket and can upload the pic they just took to Instagram in seconds.

Film and digital images are simply methods. But the art of photography is timeless. Whenever we allow a method that worked for a season to trump something timeless, we make a grave mistake. Never sacrifice the next generation on the altar of your past methods or preferences.

Now if you happen to love Sunday school, I won't judge you—but you must at least admit Sunday school is not for everyone. Actually, it's not for most people. I can back that up with statistics. According to most research, nearly 75 percent of the people in the average community will not go to church this next Sunday. And less than half of those who go to church will go to Sunday school. That means half the people who actually go to church don't even like Sunday school. Most people don't get up on Sunday morning and say, "I can't wait to go to a building, sit in class, and listen to someone teach me the Bible."

Sometimes we forget that we can't ultimately make kids go to church, learn the Bible and follow Jesus. The sobering reality is that, sooner or later, kids will grow into teenagers who will drive themselves wherever they want to go on Sunday—just like every other day of the week. So, the only thing we can consistently and predictably do is to create an environment where kids or teenagers want to show up.

Smart leaders know that just because something worked once, doesn't mean it still works. It has becoming increasingly difficult to ignore the decades of evidence that most kids grow up and grow out of a classroom model. That's why it's strange that even in recent years, curriculums have been developed and volunteers retrained to launch new and improved versions of a class approach.

Several years ago I heard Dr. Howard Hendricks, seminary professor at Dallas Theological Seminary, speak about change. He said he had been invited as a consultant to critique a specific church. After observing everything that happened in their church on Sunday and during the week he gave this report: "Unless you make some radical changes, you should just put up ropes at the front door, and charge people admission to see what church looked like 50 years ago." Dr. Hendricks was 70-plus-years-old at the time. I am sure he had seen enough recent church history to give credibility to his observation. I also suspect many of that church's staff were surprised at his response. When you have been doing something the same way for a long time, it's easy assume it's the best way to do things—especially when it works for the people who are coming. That's the reason a lot of churches will fight to defend a Sunday school model. They mistakenly justify what they are doing because of the people who *are* coming. They should consider evaluating what they are doing based on the people who *aren't yet* coming.

When it comes to creating a place for kids and teenagers, it's critical to re-evaluate and rethink your model frequently. You need to ask some hard questions related to what drives your strategy. The traditional values and practices behind most classroom models have existed for so long, they can make it hard to transition to more relational models.

When I was a young, idealistic student pastor in my first church, the teenagers complained that Sunday school was boring. So, I did what I thought was creative at the time. I stopped ordering the denominational literature, bought a book by Chuck Swindoll on understanding the Bible, redesigned the large group experience, and divided teenagers into smaller groups with leaders to have meaningful discussions. Within the first month I got a phone call from the chairman of deacons. His opening remark made me nervous: "My son told me you are no longer using the denominational quarterlies. Why is that?" I thought my reply was extremely logical: "Well, a lot of the teenagers say the denomination material is really boring, so I wanted to try something new." I will never forget how he responded: "What does boring have to do with anything? That's what we used when I was his age and look how I turned out." Soon after, I got a visit from the curriculum developers in our denomination asking me to explain my frustration with their content. It was then I learned how difficult it is to change anything that has existed in a church culture for decades.

There are a lot of incredible things someone can learn from a classroom model.
- It's important for kids and teenagers to memorize and apply core truths of Scripture.
- Gifted teachers should be recruited to communicate to kids.
- Kids should learn to navigate the overarching story of the Bible.

But we should also recognize that educating Christians is not the same thing as making disciples. We are not claiming Sunday school was never effective. We are suggesting, however, that there are better models to disciple kids in today's culture. That's why we advocate designing a model that makes relationships a priority. Everyone can define or redefine any model in their ministry to be more relational (even Sunday school). But you have to be careful that you don't put new wine in old wineskins. You need to recognize the part of your system that needs to fundamentally change before you can move on. Consider the contrast that potentially exists between a model built around relationships and a model driven to educate kids.

	SUNDAY SCHOOL	SMALL GROUPS
Goal:	Education	Spiritual Formation
Focus:	Teach Bible	Make Disciples
Model:	Classroom	Circles
Time:	Sunday Morning	When it Works Best
Priority:	Present Lesson	Dialogue and Community
Volunteers:	Recruit Teachers	Develop Leaders
Evaluation:	Church Practices	Personal Faith
Emphasis:	Knowing Scripture	Knowing God

This chart is important primarily because many churches who try to shift to a group mindset are still driven by the primary goal to educate children and teenagers.

Are we saying every Sunday school model is focused on education and not spiritual formation? No. There are always exceptions. But educating Christians tends to be the default goal of most Sunday school programs.

Are we suggesting a small group ministry should not teach the Bible? Clearly, that's not the case. As we have explained in previous chapters, we think you can actually teach Scripture *more effectively* through caring, consistent SGLs who are personally involved with the kids they lead.

There are fundamental differences between the mindset that drives a Sunday school model and the mindset that drives a small group model. So if you are transitioning to a lead small culture, remember the goal is to stimulate spiritual formation, not just teach spiritual information. There is a tendency for leaders who have been involved in Sunday school to default back to a classroom model simply because it's easier to recruit a few teachers than a host of small group leaders.

We have never claimed a small group model is easy. We just think it's worth it.

Remember this:
You don't teach kids to be disciples, you lead them to be disciples.
So, maybe kids need more leaders, not more lessons.

TRANSITION TO CIRCLES

Shifting a culture takes time. It requires effort, planning, and a lot of conversations. You may experience setbacks. You'll probably face a bit of opposition. And chances are, it will take longer than you think.

We can't tell you exactly how long it will take to make this transition in your church. The amount of time required to move to a lead small culture will be affected by a number of variables including:

The history or age of your church.
The length of time you have been a leader at your church.
The traditions or style of your church.
The size or location of your church.

We have worked with leaders who feel they shifted the culture of their church within a few months and others who feel it took a few years. A good rule of thumb is that it will probably take at least two years before your staff begins to feel like small groups are becoming a priority in your culture. Why is that? Because there is something about doing it the third time that begins to cement the value into the minds and hearts of your volunteers.

The first year, it feels like you are experimenting with a new idea.
The second year, it feels like you are improving what you learned the first year.
The third year, it feels like you are establishing a pattern or model.

There is nothing magical about a two-year mark. It's just important to realize creating a culture where everyone champions the same priorities takes time. Therefore, we have organized the transition process into three major stages to help leaders understand what's involved in transitioning a culture. Remember, the suggested time frames are only guidelines depending on your church.

In STAGE ONE of your transition to a lead small culture, you'll need to focus on gathering and sharing INFORMATION. This could take around six months.

In STAGE TWO of the transition, you'll begin the IMPLEMENTATION of what you learned in the information phase. This could take another six months to a year.

In STAGE THREE of the transition, you'll need to continue to make IMPROVEMENT in your culture. This initial process of fine-tuning will likely take another six months, but it's something you should never stop doing. Creating a culture is one thing, but sustaining it is another. As a ministry leader, you will never stop improving your culture.

Your goal, by the way, is INTEGRATION. It's what happens when the vision we've cast throughout this book becomes a reality. The goal is a church where groups are the answer for discipleship in every age group. It's a church where your structure supports groups, your leaders are empowered, and you've created better small group experiences. It's a place where every kid can belong.

When I (Reggie) wrote the book *Think Orange*, I worked with Carey Nieuwhof to outline a seven-step process for developing an integrated model of family ministry. They are the seven steps a church needs to take in order to move from where they are to where they want to be. We think these seven steps will work in moving to a lead small culture, too, which is why we've included them as a part of the three stages of transition.

So if you're ready to
Drop out of class
Do more than a concert
And go in circles,
Then you're ready to begin creating a lead small culture.

STAGE ONE: **INFORMATION**
(may take up to six months)

1. Discover
If you're just beginning to take steps toward transitioning your church, this is likely where you are now. This book is a great start. Now, continue learning, asking questions, and considering what a lead small culture might look like for your church.

Put this book, or another resource like it, into the hands of your core team so you can spark more conversations. Let these resources begin to craft a language around this issue so your team can discover and dream together. Identify a handful of ministries, comparable to yours in size or context, which have made the transition to a groups-based model, and learn from them.

Not sure where to find those leaders? Hop on your favorite social media platform and check out hashtags like #thinkorange. You'll find a large, diverse community of leaders who passionately believe small groups are the answer and who would love to have a conversation with you.

2. Define an action plan
After you've done your research and spent time thoroughly exploring ideas with your team, it's time to create a plan. Be specific. What are your next steps? How can you improve your structure, empower your leaders, and create an experience so that everything you do supports small groups? What will success look like in your ministry? Work with your team to clarify the win, and identify the shifts you need to make in order for change to happen. Do this together. It's essential for your staff to be on the same page.

3. Communicate
Communication needs to be an ongoing process if you're going to lead any kind of change in an organization. But your communication needs an additional level of intentionality after you and your team outline an action plan. There are three circles of people you need to consider.

First, discuss your plan with your core decision-makers: the people who report to you, key team members at your level, and the people you report to. When those conversations have brought more clarity to your action plan, share the results and the broad principles of your vision with the next circle, your influencers. These are key volunteers and focus groups of parents. Provide opportunities to test your ideas in partnership with them while you invite, and listen to their input. When that's done, you can begin sharing the vision and the plan with a larger crowd: the rest of your volunteers, parents, and kids.

One more thing to consider as you begin to communicate with your circles: before your culture can change, your language will need to change. Some of you may need to consider making some revisions so . . .

teachers become small group leaders.
classrooms become groups.
lesson plans become discussion questions.
their class becomes their few.

The words we speak fuel our beliefs, and our beliefs drive our behaviors. So, the more you talk about it, the more you'll become what you say you believe. Communicate and never stop.

"When we were beginning to build a lead small culture, we had to fight the mentality that volunteers were merely 'babysitters' instead of small group leaders. We had to lead up, and change our vocabulary." – **Bobbi Miller** (Elementary)

"As a youth pastor in a church tradition where we were accustomed to having a 'rock star' personality, this new model was difficult for some to envision. The first thing I did was to get buy-in from our senior pastor. When he was on board, he spoke about it and affirmed the vision from the pulpit. Then I met with our Christian education pastor to reorganize some of our programming so that, together, we could cultivate a culture of small groups throughout our entire church." – **Jeffrey Wallace** (High School)

STAGE TWO: **IMPLEMENTATION**
(six months to one year)

4. Reorganize
Now is the time for action. Begin reassigning your staff, budget, programs, volunteers, and resources to support small groups. It's possible you'll need to add something or someone to your structure, but it's also likely you'll need to redefine, reallocate, and subtract.

Remember, you may need to stop doing some things that are successful if you want to make groups more successful.
There may even be a few people who will opt to leave rather than make the transition with you. That's okay. Acknowledge and celebrate the success of where your ministry has been, but stay focused on where you want to go. Patiently and consistently remind people where you are headed and why.

5. Develop

As you reorganize, you'll need to invest extra time training your staff, your small group leaders, and your other volunteer teams. It's not enough to just develop new strategies or structures. You've got to develop people.

Remember, the *what* and *how* of someone's job is helpful and informative, but the *why* will inspire them. Develop your staff and volunteers by clarifying the win for your ministry and training them in light of their contribution to that win.

6. Promote

How will you promote this new direction to your church in larger ways and from multiple platforms? Consider a strategic message series, your social media channels, or your church's existing promotional channels. Share stories, cast vision, and dream out loud in a way that ignites passion in people. Then watch it spread.

7. Launch

Some leaders launch too quickly, before the vision for groups has spread or before the structure exists to support them. Others think and plan for years, but never launch. You aren't that leader. Launch well. Take your time with the first six steps in this process, but don't neglect to set a start date. Prepare your team, your volunteers, and your families . . . but then *start!*

STAGE THREE: **IMPROVEMENT**
(six months to forever)

Shortly after your launch, you'll see areas that need improvement. You might see them *minutes* after your first week when well-meaning and critically constructive leaders start giving you feedback.

Every structure needs to be improved. Your leaders will always need more training. Your small group experiences will never stop needing some adjustments. So, if you get some of that critical feedback, that's okay. It's part of the process. Keep improving, keep tweaking, keep making things better.

Remember how my church handed me (Elle) thirty girls to disciple when I first became a small group leader? That wasn't perfect. But we didn't need to be perfect in the beginning. We just needed to begin.

"It took me three years to make the transition. We did it one grade at a time, beginning with the oldest kids. We let that group become a pilot group for the others and we bragged on them endlessly so other groups would get excited about following in their footsteps."
– **Sue Miller** (Preschool/Elementary)

"We also started our transition by using one grade as an experiment. By doing it one grade level at a time, we were able to minimize the number of small group leaders we needed to recruit before we launched. This allowed us to lead the transition slowly throughout our ministry, rather than forcing a huge overnight change."
– **Cass Brannan** (Preschool)

"There will be a number of things you'll want to accomplish, but you've got to prioritize the things you need to improve. When we began our transition, we really needed three great storytellers for our large group environment. But we knew we needed small group leaders more. So for six months, we put off our storyteller recruitment, used videos instead of live communicators, and focused instead on recruiting new small group leaders." – **Gina McClain** (Elementary)

"When I took my job, there was very little consistency with our volunteers. The idea of finding SGLs to serve every week for every kid was more than I could even wrap my head around. So, we started by asking leaders to begin serving every *other* week with the same group of kids. Then we staggered volunteers so that, even though we couldn't yet give kids the same leader every week, we could at least give them two leaders who alternated weeks. Is that the dream? No. But, today, almost three years later, we have more leaders than ever who are bought into the vision and have *asked* to become every-week leaders. To get here, we had to be flexible in the beginning. We had to meet our volunteers where they were, and lead them to where we wanted them to go." – **Jenny Zimmer** (Preschool)

Transitioning a culture is possible.

We can't tell you exactly when it will happen, but it *will* happen if you never stop improving and working toward your goal.

THE GOAL: **INTEGRATION**

> "You won't always be able to see a culture change. You'll just realize it has."
> – **Tom Shefchunas** (Middle School)

Remember, unless you know what you're transitioning to, you may not really be transitioning. Ultimately, you don't just want to see a lead small culture happen in the age-group ministry you happen to care about. If your church is going to become a place where every kid belongs, a lead small culture must exist in every age-group ministry in your church. So, we wanted to give you a snapshot of what an integrated lead small culture looks like. (If you skimmed the rest of the book, this is your summary.)

From time to time, you may need to do a quick ministry inventory to evaluate your lead small culture. Use these nine statements to catalyze discussion. Invite core leaders on your team to assign a number to each statement and see where you need to improve.

GAUGE KEY:

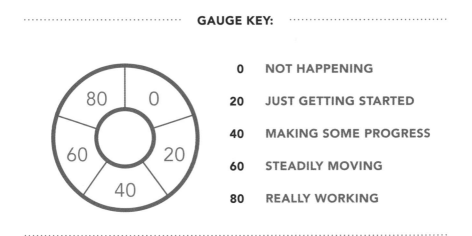

0	**NOT HAPPENING**
20	**JUST GETTING STARTED**
40	**MAKING SOME PROGRESS**
60	**STEADILY MOVING**
80	**REALLY WORKING**

IMPROVE THE STRUCTURE

1. ◯ A designated leader and team meet regularly to coordinate the small group strategy.

2. ◯ You evaluate and tweak your ministry programs so they are steps to groups.

3. ◯ Your seasonal and weekly calendar complements what happens in the culture and at home.

EMPOWER THE LEADER

1. ◯ The majority of your small group leaders have shifted to a weekly responsibility.

2. ◯ You do something every week to thank, encourage, and equip your SGLs.

3. ◯ There is a clear ongoing strategy for how you recruit and apprentice SGLs.

CREATE THE EXPERIENCE

1. ◯ Resources and curriculum support SGLs with what they need this week.

2. ◯ The physical space is designed and managed to help the small group win.

3. ◯ Everyone understands how to evaluate the small group relationships and experience.

You will never be done improving your structure.
You will probably never have all the SGLs you need.
You can usually do something more to improve your weekly experiences.

Maybe that's why it's harder—not easier—to create a lead small culture.
It will be messy, because relationships are messy. People are messy.

Someone will probably get mad.

It will take longer than you think.

And you will never be done.

But it will be worth it

Why will it be worth it?

Because kids need to be known.

Every kid needs to be known before they can feel **welcome**.
Every kid needs to be known before they can feel **forgiven**.
Every kid needs to be known before they can know they **belong**.

AUTHOR BIOS

REGGIE JOINER

Reggie Joiner is the founder and CEO of Orange, a non-profit organization whose purpose is to influence those who influence the next generation. Orange provides resources and training for churches and organizations that create environments for parents, kids and teenagers. Prior to Orange, Joiner co-founded North Point Community Church in Alpharetta, GA, with Andy Stanley. During his 11 years as the executive director of family ministry, he developed a new concept for relevant ministry for children, teenagers, and married adults. If you end up road tripping with him across the country on Orange Tour, be prepared to stop at every antique store along the way. He has found a way to wear orange for 3,453 days and counting.

Joiner has authored and co-authored books including, *Think Orange, The Think Orange Handbook, Zombies, Football, and the Gospel, Seven Practices of Effective Ministry, Parenting Beyond Your Capacity, Lead Small,* and *Creating a Lead Small Culture.*

Joiner and his wife Debbie live in Cumming, GA, and have four children: Reggie Paul, Hannah, Sarah, and Rebekah. For more information about Reggie Joiner, visit ReggieJoiner.com or follow him on Twitter @ReggieJoiner.

KRISTEN IVY

Kristen Ivy is executive director of messaging at Orange. Before beginning her career at the company in 2006, she was a high school biology and English teacher, where she learned first hand the joy and importance of influencing the next generation. She received her Master of Divinity in 2009. At Orange, Ivy has played an integral role in the evolution of the preschool, middle school, high school and curriculum and has shared her experiences at speaking events across the country. Ivy is co-author of *Playing For Keeps*, and *Creating a Lead Small Culture*. She is a collegiate cheerleading captain, turned theologian whose dream is to star in Cirque du Soleil.

Ivy lives in Cumming, GA, with her husband Matt, and her two children, Sawyer and Hensley. For more information about Kristen Ivy, visit KristenIvy.com or follow her on Twitter @Kristen_Ivy.

ELLE CAMPBELL

Elle Campbell is the middle school small group coordinator at The Chapel at CrossPoint in Buffalo, NY. In addition, she also develops lead small and middle school ministry content for Orange. Campbell is co-author of Creating a Lead Small Culture. She and her husband Kenny are the creators and operators of their website, Stuff You Can Use, to provide resources for youth pastors. Campbell is an expert at finding sloth YouTube videos and clearing 10 inches of snow off her car with a butter knife. For more information about Elle Campbell, follow her on Twitter @Ellllllllllle (with eleven l's) or visit ElleCampbell.org.